Jung the Philosopher

NEW STUDIES IN AESTHETICS

Robert Ginsberg
General Editor

Vol. 3

PETER LANG
New York • Bern • Frankfurt am Main • Paris

Marian L. Pauson

Jung the Philosopher

Essays in Jungian Thought

PETER LANG
New York • Bern • Frankfurt am Main • Paris

Library of Congress Cataloging-in-Publication Data

Pauson, Marian L.
    Jung the philosopher : essays in Jungian
thought / Marian L. Pauson.
        p. cm. — (New studies in aesthetics ; vol. 3)
        Bibliography: p.
        Includes index.
        1. Jung, C. G. (Carl Gustav). 1875-1961 —
Philosophy.   I. Title.   II. Series: New studies in
aesthetics ; v. 3.
B4651.J84P38   1988   193—dc19   88-5388
ISBN 0-8204-0586-8   CIP
ISSN 0893-6005

CIP-Titelaufnahme der Deutschen Bibliothek

Pauson, Marian L.:
Jung the philosopher : essays in Jungian thought
/ Marian L. Pauson. — New York; Bern; Frank-
furt am Main; Paris: Lang, 1988.
  (New Studies in Aesthetics; Vol. 3)
  ISBN 0-8204-0586-8

NE: GT

Printed by Weihert-Druck GmbH, Darmstadt, West Germany

To My Mother

TABLE OF CONTENTS

INTRODUCTION xi

CHAPTER

1 PHILOSOPHICAL BEGINNINGS:

 C. G. Jung's Philosophical Mentors 1

2 THE BASIS OF KNOWLEDGE:

 C. G. Jung and the *A Priori* 13

3 THE IMPACT OF HUMAN CONSCIOUSNESS ON
 THE DYNAMICS OF THE WORLD:

 Synchronicity: An Acausal Concept for
  Contemporary Metaphysics 31

4 HUMAN CREATIVITY IN ART AND LIFE:
 C. G. Jung's Philosophy of Creativity 45

5 HUMAN LIFE AS CONSCIOUSNESS AND MORAL
 ACTION:
 Imagination and Life 61

6 THE PROBLEM OF EVIL:

 Jung and Plotinus on Evil 79

7 THE ROOTS OF SYMBOLIC FORMS:

 Structures in Art Media 91

8 FOUNDATIONS OF EDUCATION:

 C. G. Jung's Topology and Its Educational
  Implications 107

9   EDUCATION FOR THE MATURER YEARS:

   C. G. Jung on Education for the Second
      Half of Life 123

10   BEYOND THE RATIONAL:

   Jung and Mysticism 133

11   STAGES IN THE CREATIVE PROCESS:

   The Seven Days of Creation 145

CONCLUSION 189

BIBLIOGRAPHY 205

ABOUT THE ILLUSTRATORS 225

INDEX 227

LIST OF ILLUSTRATIONS

Mandala, by Henry Reed   21

Shifting Shapes Fuse Space-Time, by Fay Zetlin   30

Medieval Church Structures, by Betty Burke   102

The Seven Days of Creation, by Lorraine Fink:
  Let there be light   146

  Let there be a firmament   154

  Let the earth put forth vegetation   160

  Let there be lights in the firmament   166

  God created the great sea monsters   172

  Male and female created he them   176

  The heavens and the earth were finished   182

INTRODUCTION

> Philosophy cannot be content with analyz-
> ing the individual forms of human culture.
> It seeks a universal synthetic view which
> includes all individual forms.
>
> Ernst Cassirer, *An Essay on Man*

While philosophers today are often busy tidying their houses of thought through contemporary techniques of analysis, many of the enduring questions traditionally left to philosophers go unanswered: questions which challenge human speculation at the frontiers of knowledge. However, philosophy, or "love of wisdom," as synthesis of all areas of learning is a task for which few scholars today are prepared. Few individuals are able to cover a sufficiently broad spectrum of knowledge in one lifetime while gifted with sufficient speculative insight to attempt such a task.

C. G. Jung is one such person: physician and psychotherapist by profession, student of anthropology, mythology, philosophy, religion, and other areas of learning by avocation, as well as lecturer, teacher, prolific author, and, despite his claims to the contrary, a speculative philosopher.

Jung's inquiring mind searched for knowledge wherever his curiosity led him. Yet in all his learning, he was actively involved in the human world through his profession of psychotherapy. Thus his world view, his synthesis, does not rest on a lofty speculative plane, but rather is grounded in a day to day relationship with human beings, with the problems and difficulties of individuals seeking health, fulfillment, and meaning in their lives.

Finding meaning in an individual life is the key to Jung's psychotherapy known as individuation. Through meaning lies the possibility of higher consciousness and morality in the truest sense. In Jung's synthesis, meaning is linked to the discovery of the Self, the irrational giver of all experience. Within this perspective, to know is to bring one's conscious ego life into harmony with the Self; herein lies one's purpose as well as one's happiness and peace. Every individual, like every leaf or flower, is different. Every individual has a history and a unique dimension in the universe. To know oneself, the individual must go beyond collective norms and pressures to conformity; the individual must discover what makes one different, not in a superficial way, but in the most intimate psychological sense. Jung believed that humanity knows very little about the human psyche and that his own psychology barely scratched the surface of human understanding.

Jung was aware, however, as many psychologists and philosophers are not, that all psychologies are rooted in philosophical presuppositions, namely in accepted givens about humanity and the world, which underlie the bases of all psychological hypotheses, and that all philosophies likewise are grounded in psychological orientations, that is, in the psychological temperament of the philosopher. No wonder that until the twentieth century, philosophy and psychology were of the same discipline!

Today many philosophers are preoccupied with the language in which philosophical questions are formulated, thereby evading the heart of the questions. They might look more deeply, however, into their own psychological expectation that to understand the language is to dismiss the question. A preoccupation with linguistic analysis, however beneficial for intellectual housekeeping, can never erase the human sense of wonder and the inner light of consciousness ever reflecting itself. If through analysis one throws away all the furniture of the mind, new furniture must then be created. The new furniture, the new language, will arise as did the old out of human beings in their unique metaphoric confrontation with the cosmos.

C.G. Jung realized that the languages of the varied disciplines available to him in his time to explain the human psyche were inadequate; they did not sufficiently illuminate the experiences of his patients, nor of himself. Consequently, he searched in the broad history of human culture for the images and the words, for the continuity and the perspective, to shed light on the deeper problems of his time. In doing so, he emerged not only as a healer of individuals, a psychotherapist, but also as a philosopher.

While Jung the psychotherapist is well known, Jung the philosopher is not. Hence the reason for this book. Jung's philosophy is interwoven with his psychology; yet he was aware of his presuppositions in both fields and made no apologies for them. He did not claim to have created an absolute system but only to have put forth his myth. Likewise, this book does not claim to set forth final answers to philosophical questions but only to present Jung's point of view, his answers. Part of Jung's legacy lies in his *Collected Works*. Here among the multi-faceted dimensions of his thought and research, among the case histories and intricate studies of esoteric symbology, one can also discover his philosophical ideas, his answers to the enduring questions.

What, then, is Jung's contribution to speculative philosophy? Where does his philosophy begin? What does he say about the basis of knowledge? the impact of human consciousness on the dynamics of the world as process? human creativity in art and life? human life as consciousness and moral action? the problem of evil? the origins of symbolic forms? the foundations of education? education for the maturer years? life after death?

The task of this book is to answer these questions. Most of the chapters originate as professional papers or articles, and all represent an effort to present Jung's speculative thought to the philosophic community.

CHAPTER 1

PHILOSOPHICAL BEGINNINGS:

C. G. Jung's Philosophical Mentors

Who are C. G. Jung's philosophical mentors? To whom does he owe his ideas, his concepts, his words? To ask such questions is to approach Jung's synthesis in a purely causal way and to see creative genius in general as a type of linear process of borrowing, adding, compounding, and synthesizing, with nothing new in the real sense of the word. Such an attitude is anathema to the very essence of creativity, as Jung himself lived it and wrote about it. He said, "My life has been in a sense the quintessence of what I have written, not the other way around. The way I am and the way I write are a unity. All my ideas and all my endeavors are myself.[1] However, this self, according to Jung, is essentially an inner experience: "I can understand myself only in the light of inner happenings";[2] Only what is interior has proved to have substance and a determining value."[3] Jung claimed that his writings were himself and that this self was essentially an inner experience; the outer aspects of his life were, as he said, accidental. To speak of Jung's philosophical orientation, then, is to speak of his essential being. From Jung's point of view, to say he borrowed ideas from other philosophers in the sense that his ideas originated in the study of philosophy would be a mistake. Instead, Jung's inner experiences, his dreams, his intuitions, and his reflections were the ultimate sources of his thought. However, in his study of philosophy, as he tells us in his autobiography, he found the confirmation of his intuitions and, one might add, the verbal structures through which he gave them form. He tells of his encounters with the works of earlier thinkers and of the way his speculation accepted or rejected them.

From earliest childhood, Jung's inner experiences and his questions concerning the nature of God and the problem of evil led his path of inquiry through the books available in his father's library. Here, he rejected the theological dogmatic treatises found in a parson's study, for they did not explain his enigmatic experiences of God. His mother suggested that he read Goethe's *Faust,* which he said "poured into my soul like a miraculous balm."[4] Goethe became in his eyes a prophet, for he saw evil and its universal power in a way that defied the dogmatists. Through Goethe Jung became acquainted with philosophy, but the only philosophical reference available in his father's library was "Krug's General Dictionary of the Philosophical Sciences," second edition, 1833. Here, however, his interest in the nature of God and the question of evil found no answers.

According to his autobiography, Jung's next acquaintance with philosophy came in his late teens when he began systematically pursuing questions he had consciously framed. He read a brief introduction to the history of philosophy and found to his gratification that many of his intuitions had historical analogues. He was attracted to the thought of Pythagoras, Heraclitus, Empedocles, and Plato, but all of these ideas, while beautiful and academic, seemed remote. Only in Meister Eckhart did he feel the breath of life. The Schoolmen left him more lifeless than a desert. He wrote, "They all want to force something to come out by tricks of logic, something they have not been granted and do not really know about. They want to prove a belief to themselves, whereas actually it is a matter of experience."[5]

At this time, the critical philosophy of the eighteenth century did not appeal to him. Of the nineteenth-century philosophers, he found Hegel's language "arrogant and laborious." To him, Hegel "seemed like a man who was caged in the edifice of his own words and was pompously gesticulating in his prison."[6]

In Schopenhauer, however, he discovered his "great find," for he was the first to speak of the suffering of the world and of confusion, passion, evil—all those things which the others hardly noticed and always tried to resolve into all embracing harmony and comprehensibility. While Schopenhauer's somber picture of the world had Jung's undivided approval, his solution of the problem did not. He was disappointed by Schopenhauer's theory that the intellect need only confront the blind Will with its image in order to cause it to reverse itself. If the Will was blind, how could it see this image? And what was the intellect, but a function of the human soul?

However, Jung was impelled to study Schopenhauer more thoroughly, and he became increasingly impressed by the latter's relation to Kant. He read Kant's *Critique of Pure Reason* and thought he had discovered here the fundamental flaw in Schopenhauer's system: "He had committed the deadly sin of hypostatizing a metaphysical assertion, and of endowing a mere noumenon, a *Ding an sich,* with special qualities."[7] This illumination from Kant's theory of knowledge was for Jung even greater than Schopenhauer's "pessimistic" view of the world.

Jung recounts that this period of philosophical development extended from his seventeenth year until well into the years of his medical studies. As he grew older and before his choice of a profession, Jung found his interests drawing him in different directions: he was powerfully attracted by science, with its truths based on facts; and on the other hand, he was fascinated by everything to do with comparative religion. In the sciences he was drawn principally to zoology, paleontology, and geology; and in the humanities to Greco-Roman, Egyptian, and prehistoric archeology. In science the concrete facts and their historical background appealed to him, while in comparative religion he found the spiritual problems into which philosophy also entered. However, Jung said, "In science I missed the factor of meaning; and in religion, that of empiricism."[8]

During his Gymnasium years at Basel where he was drawn

into the intellectual-theological discussions of his uncle, a clergyman, Jung's scientific knowledge, though meager, took the lead. He
became thoroughly saturated with the scientific materialism of the
time, which for him was only painfully held in check by the evidence
of history and by Kant's *Critique of Pure Reason*. His scientific
interests were the dominant reason for his choice of medicine as a
career; yet the deeper side of his personality regarded Goethe as his
"godfather and authority," and *Faust* meant more to him than the
beloved Gospel according to St. John.

At the end of the second semester at the University of Basel, he
came in contact with spiritualism through the library of the father of
a classmate. Names like Friedrich Zoellner and William Crookes
impressed themselves on him. He also read Kant's *Dreams of a Spirit
Seer,* as well as Karl Duprel who had evaluated these ideas philosophically and psychologically. He read K.A. von Eschenmayer, J.K.
Passavant, Justinus Kerner, J. von Gorres, and several volumes of
Emanuel Swedenborg.

During his clinical semesters, he studied Kant only on Sundays.
He also read Eduard von Hartmann assiduously but felt he was not
sufficiently prepared for Nietszche who was very much discussed at
the time, mostly in adverse terms, by the allegedly competent philosophy students. Jakob Burckhardt was the supreme critical authority.

He finally read Nietszche's *Thoughts Out of Season* and carried
away by enthusiasm soon afterwards read *Thus Spake Zarathustra*.
Jung saw Nietszche's *Zarathustra* as Goethe's *Faust*. It was a tremendous experience for him, but he also saw a warning in the
bombastic language, the piling up of metaphors, the hymnlike
rapture—all a vain attempt to catch the ear of a world which had
sold its soul for a mass of disconnected facts. He wrote: "Just as *Faust*
has opened a door for me, Zarathustra slammed one shut, and it
remained shut for a long time to come."[9]

Later, in assessing the value of modern philosophy in relation to his analysis of psychological types, Jung saw Nietszche's Zarathustra as the best example of the intuitive method of grasping a problem in a non-intellectual yet philosophical way. He saw Nietszche as freeing himself from the bonds of intellect in shaping his philosophical ideas—so much so that his intuition carried him outside the bounds of a purely philosophical system and led to the creation of a work of art which is largely inaccessible to philosophical criticism. He saw Schopenhauer and Hegel as forerunners of Nietszche's intuitive approach: Schopenhauer because his intuitive feelings had such a decisive influence on Jung's thinking and Hegel because of the intuitive ideas that underlie his whole system. In both cases, Jung saw intuition subordinated to intellect, but with Nietszche intuition ranked above intellect.[10] Jung's assessment of Nietszche's use of intuition might well apply as a description of his own method and work later developed as a creative effort outside the bounds of a purely philosophical system.

However, this insight of Jung regarding Nietszche was to emerge in his development when, along with his study of William James, Henri Bergson, and others, he sought a broader understanding of the way in which philosophical methods and orientations are influenced by psychological temperament.

Let us continue the chronology of Jung's intellectual development as recorded in his autobiography: in the years of Jung's apprenticeship at the Burghölzli Mental Hospital in Zurich, Freud became vitally important to him, especially because of Freud's fundamental researches into the psychology of hysteria and of dreams. Freud introduced psychology into psychiatry, although Freud himself was a neurologist.

Between the years 1905 and 1913, Jung lectured as a professor at the University of Zurich on the psychology of primitives, on hypnosis, on the theories of Pierre Janet and Theodore Flournoy, and on Freudian psychoanalysis. During this time he also began to study mythology with a view toward understanding latent psychosis. Joseph Breuer, Freud and Janet provided him with a wealth of suggestions and stimuli.

However, it was Jung's own dreams which brought his greatest insights and vital connections to the history of culture. He said, "When I thought about dreams and the contents of the unconscious, I never did so without making historical comparisons; in my student days I always used Krug's old dictionary of philosophy. I was especially familiar with the writers of the eighteenth and early nineteenth century."[11] His dreams pointed to the foundations of cultural history and successive layers of consciousness, as well as to a collective *a priori* beneath the personal psyche. Nevertheless, he attributed to Freud's evaluation of dreams the initial demonstration of an unconscious psyche which hitherto had existed only as a philosophical postulate, in particular in the philosophies of C.G. Carus and Eduard von Hartmann.

In 1918-19, Jung began drawing mandalas which corresponded to his situation at the time. He said, "My mandalas were cryptograms concerning the state of the self which were presented to me anew each day. In them I saw the self—that is, my whole being—actually at work."[12] The self, he thought, represents the monad and corresponds to the microscopic nature of the psyche. The term "monad" suggests Liebniz's metaphysics with which Jung was well acquainted. However, Jung used the term in reference to the dynamics of the self in quite a different way, avoiding the notions of strict causality and pre-established harmony.

The understanding of the self as monad was complemented in Jung's conception by the Taoist notion of the union of opposites. In 1928, through Richard Wilhelm, Jung became acquainted with the Taoist-alchemical treatise entitled, *The Secret of the Golden Flower,* about which he wrote, "I devoured the manuscript at once, for the text gave me undreamed-of-confirmation of my ideas, about the mandala and the circumambulation of the centre."[13] Jung interpreted the Taoist notion of the union of opposites as the union of consciousness and the unconscious through surrender to a superior or divine factor. He came to understand the self as the principle and archetype of orientation and meaning wherein lies its healing function. Out of this insight emerged a first inkling of his personal myth.

These philosophical conceptions followed upon an extended period of time during which Jung had undergone his own confrontation with the unconscious. He wrote, "On August 1 the world war broke out. Now my task was clear: I had to try to understand what had happened and to what extent my own experience coincided with that of mankind in general. Therefore my first obligation was to probe the depths of my own psyche."[14] During this period of inundation from the unconscious, the incessant stream of fantasies confronted Jung as an alien world; yet he deliberately committed himself to this dangerous enterprise in order, among other reasons, to understand the world of his patients: "....I was well aware that the so-called helper—that is, myself—could not help them unless he knew their fantasy material from his own direct experience, and that at present all he possessed were a few theoretical prejudices of dubious value."[15] Later Jung said that the years when he was pursuing his inner images were the most important in his life and that in them everything essential was decided. The later details were only supplements and clarifications of the material that burst forth from the unconscious during this time.

In order to clarify his inner experiences, Jung sought for their historical prefiguration, asking himself, "Where have my particular premises already occurred in history?"[16] He felt that if he had not succeeded in finding such evidence, he never would have been able to substantiate his ideas. He believed that psychology more than any other natural science was subject to the personal bias of the observer and that therefore the psychologist must depend in the highest degree upon historical and literary parellels if one wishes to exclude at least the crudest errors in judgment. In particular, Jung's encounter with alchemy provided him with an historical basis, a natural bridge between Gnosticism and neo-Platonism on the one hand and modern psychology and the unconscious on the other. Jung had been drawn initially to Gnosticism because in accordance with his own intuitions it introduced the higher feminine principle which he had found lacking in Freud's psychology.[17]

In alchemy Jung saw the historical counterpart of his psychology of the unconscious and the possibility of an uninterrupted chain back to Gnosticism. When he poured over old texts dating back to the sixteenth century, everything fell into place: the fantasy-images, the empirical material he had gathered in his practice, and the conclusions he had drawn from it. He saw what psychic contents meant when seen in historical perspective, and his understanding of their typical character already begun with the investigation of myths was deepened. The primordial images and the nature of the archetypes took a central place in his researches, and he saw that without history no psychology was possible and certainly no psychology of the unconscious.

His concept of the self as the archetype of orientation and meaning, which unites consciousness and the unconscious through surrender to a divine factor, was related not only to the notion of tao but to the most primitive conceptions of divine energy. Jung saw the concept of tao, which is usually associated with Lao-Tzu, 604 B.C., as older than Lao-Tzu and bound up with the ancient folk religion of Taoism, the "way of Heaven," a concept corresponding to the Vedic *rta*. He believed that the affinity of tao with Brahmanic ideas, while unmistakable, does not necessarily imply direct contact, for the primordial image underlying both rta-brahman-atman and tao is as universal as humanity, appearing in every age and among all people as a primitive conception of energy, or "soul force." For example, he saw in his own time Bergson's unending *durée créatrice* as a modern conception of this irrational, inconceivable union of opposites. Knowledge of tao has the same redeeming and uplifting effects as the knowledge of Brahman.[18]

Tao as the creative process begets as the father and brings forth as the mother. It is the beginning and end of all creatures. Being one with tao resembles the state of infancy, a psychological attitude which in Christianity is essential for obtaining the kingdom of heaven. "Unless ye become as little children, ye shall not enter the kingdom of heaven" (Matthew 18:3). In Christianity, through this irrational symbol, the childlike attitude, the redeeming effect comes. Jung held that while the Christian symbol has a more social character than the related conceptions of the East, nevertheless both are directly connected with age-old dynamic ideas of a magical power emanating from people and things—or at a higher level of development—from gods or a divine principle.[19] In Jung's psychology, submission to this higher power associated with the central archetype of the Self brings about reconciliation of the opposite dynamic forces of consciousness and the unconscious.

In this brief overview of Jung's philosophical mentors, one can see that the conceptions deriving from his own inner experiences have their progenitors not only in the history of philosophy but in the history of religion and culture as well. The historic symbolic forms through which he discovered deeper layers of meaning in his own images were not restricted to Western culture, nor to any particular period of philosophy.

Among Jung's basic philosophical concepts underlying the notion of the self, two of the most important are the notions of the collective unconscious and the archetypes, which Jung first came to through his own dreams and reflections. However, he also found in his study of philosophy historical counterparts. Surely the concepts of the world soul and the Forms in Plato's thought and in the neo-Platonism underlying Gnosticism are progenitors. The archetypes, like the forms, structure both the world and humanity. However, for Jung, unlike Plato and the whole neo-Platonic tradition, there is no pure realm of the Forms, that is, of the archetypes in the strict intellectual/spiritual sense. The archetypes manifest themselves as energies structuring human emotions and fantasies, and through affect these energies reach consciousness. As structuring energies, the archetypes are manifested in inner and outer life with a simultaneity which Jung came to view as meaningful coincidence or, to use his later term, synchronicity. The dynamics of Jung's world view reflects Einstein's notion of relativity; the *unus mundus,* the unitary world, includes both psyche and matter. These conceptions Jung developed more fully in later life, relying on notions in modern physics. He was especially interested in the archetype of number as primordial structuring principle of humanity and the universe; in this regard, the work of Wolfgang Pauli on the "psychophysical" problem was of importance to him. With Pauli he co-authored "The Interpretation of Nature and the Psyche," 1955.[20]

For Jung, however, the great mystery was consciousness itself; for him consciousness creates the world: "...man is indispensable for the completion of creation; ...in fact, he himself is the second creator of the world, who alone has given to the world objective existence—without which, unheard, unseen, silently eating, giving birth, dying, heads nodding through hundreds of millions of years; it would have gone on in the profoundest night of non-being down to its unknown end. Human consciousness created objective existence and meaning, and man found his indispensable place in the great process of being."[21] Here Jung's thoughts are close to Ernst Cassirer's, but they came to him while alone in Africa in the savannah watching silent herds of animals. In this profound moment, he realized his myth, his purpose.

In conclusion, to pose a critical question regarding the origins of Jung's ideas as he himself has revealed these origins is to go beyond Jung and to ask: whence the source of human knowledge? This is a basic question of epistemology, one for philosophers to debate. However, Jung himself claimed that all of his ideas and all of his endeavors were himself. In his autobiography, he portrays the unfolding of these ideas in the context of his own inner experiences, his work, his study, his reflections. While one can find threads of his thought in earlier thinkers and in contemporary conceptions, one cannot reduce his creative genius, his synthesis, his "myth," to any one source.

12

CHAPTER 1

All references to C. G. Jung's works, unless otherwise indicated, are taken from the *Collected Works* (C. W.) second edition, 20 vols., Princeton University Press.

1. C. G. Jung, *Memories, Dreams, Reflections,* recorded and edited by Aniela Jaffé, translated from the German by Richard and Clara Winston (New York: Vintage Books, 1963), xii.
2. *Ibid.* 5
3. *Ibid.* ix.
4. *Ibid.* 60.
5. *Ibid.* 69.
6. *Ibid.*
7. *Ibid.* 70.
8. *Ibid.* 72.
9. *Ibid.* 103.
10. "The Type Problem in Modern Philosophy" (1920), C. W., 6:320-321 (540).
11. *Memories, Dreams, Reflections,* 161.
12. *Ibid.* 196.
13. *Ibid.* 197.
14. *Ibid.* 176.
15. *Ibid.* 178-179.
16. *Ibid.* 200.
17. *Ibid.* n. 201.
18. "The Type Problem in Poetry" (1923), C. W., 6:214-215 (358-362).
19. *Ibid* 216 (365)
20. C. G. Jung and W. Pauli, *The Interpretation of Nature and the Psyche* (New York: Pantheon, 1955; London: Routledge and Kegan Paul, 1955).
21. *Memories, Dreams, Reflections,* 256.

CHAPTER 2

THE BASIS OF KNOWLEDGE:

C. G. Jung and the *A Priori**

The term "a priori" is taken from Kant and has a special meaning in his system of thought, but the problem of the *a priori*— what is first in the order of knowledge—takes varied forms in the thinking of contemporary philosophers. For example, the question of what is first is manifested in the problem of "the given," which has been formulated by men such as C.I. Lewis, Hans Reichenbach, Everett W. Hall,[1] and others. The question of what is first also comes up in the study of basic philosophical metaphors. For example, the American philosopher Max Black[2] and the French phenomenologist Mikel Dufrenne,[3] among others, have probed the basis of rudimentary philosophical conceptions in their linguistic studies of models and metaphors. Their thinking gives rise to questions such as this: if the study of philosophical metaphors and scientific models takes us beyond model and metaphor to their origins in creative acts of genius, to what structural basis, then, can we look for the grounding of our conceptual world or even our linguistic world? To these and other epistemological questions, as well as those concerning the foundations of logical systems, Carl G. Jung's though may be illuminating.

One usually thinks of Jung in terms of depth psychology and aesthetics. Jung has much to contribute to these areas of speculation, particularly in his conception of the archetypes, but another dimension of Jung's thought touches upon the more abstract level of

*First published in Tulane *Studies in Philosophy: Epistemology II,* XVIII, 1969.

philosophical conception. I shall explore this level in a consideration of Jung's *a priori*.

Jung refers to Kant in using the term "a priori," and some aspects of Jung's thought coincide with Kantian thinking. Let us, then, take cognizance of the term as Kant uses it. At the very beginning of the Introduction to the *Critique of Pure Reason,* Kant uses the term *"a priori"* in both the first and second editions. In Norman Kemp Smith's translation (1961), we find these passages:

> A (or first) edition: Such universal modes of knowledge, which at the same time possess the character of inner necessity, must in themselves, independently of experience, be clear and certain. They are therefore entitled knowledge *a priori;* whereas, on the other hand, that which is borrowed solely from experience, is, as we say, known only *a posteriori,* or empirically.

> B (or second) edition: In what follows, therefore, we shall understand by *a priori* knowledge, not knowledge independent of this or that experience, but knowledge absolutely independent of all experience. Opposed to it is empirical knowledge, which is knowledge possible only *a posteriori,* that is, through experience.[4]

In the *Critique of Pure Reason* Kant delineates this elaborate *a priori,* these necessary modes of human knowledge. In Kant's system the products of knowledge, or the "objects" of knowledge, if we may use that term, are phenomena and noumena, and, due to the mind's peculiar cognitive structure, phenomena and noumena remain in an irreconcilable dualism. Although Kant's later works, *The Critique of Practical Reason* and *The Critique of Judgment* integrate moral and aesthetic experience to his theory of knowledge, this dualism remains. In Jung's epistemology, however, a unity of opposites stems from his conception of the *a priori*. This unity is especially manifested in Jung's analysis of uniting symbols. Let us now take the term *"a priori"* as it appears in Jung's writings.

In "The Role of the Unconscious" Jung refers to the Kantian categories in his use of the term *"a priori"*:

> It should on no account be imagined that
> there are such things as *inherited ideas*. Of
> that there can be no question. There are,
> however, innate possibilities of ideas, *a priori*
> conditions for fantasy-production which are
> somewhat similar to the Kantian categories.
> Though these innate conditions do not pro-
> duce any contents of themselves, they give
> definite form to the contents that have
> already been acquired.[5]

In the following passage from *Archetypes and the Collective Unconscious,* Jung expands the notion to include performed patterns of apperception:

> It is in my view a great mistake to suppose
> that the psyche of a new-born child is a
> *tabula rasa* in the sense that there is abso-
> lutely nothing in it. In so far as the child is
> born with a differentiated brain that is
> predetermined by heredity and therefore

individualized, it meets sensory stimuli coming from outside not with any aptitudes, but
with *specific* ones, and this necessarily results
in a particular, individual choice and pattern
of apperception. These aptitudes can be
shown to be inherited instincts and preformed patterns, the latter being the *a priori*
and formal conditions of apperception that
are based on instinct. Their presence gives
the world of the child and the dreamer its
anthropmorphic stamp...It is not, therefore,
a question of inherited *ideas* but of inherited
possibilities of ideas. Nor are they individual
acquisitions but, in the main common to all,
as can be seen from the universal occurrences of the archetypes.[6]

Jung does not deny that there is a world of realty, a world of
objects with which the mind, or the psyche, interacts in the order of
knowing. He rather insists that though there are objects which we
perceive, nevertheless our very perception is conditioned by the *a
priori* structure of the psyche. This situation is particularly evident
in the study of the primitive's perception of objects:

Primitive man's perception of objects is conditioned only partly by the objective behavior
of things themselves, whereas a much greater
part is often played by intrapsyche facts
which are not related to external objects
except by way of projection. This is due to
the simple fact that the primitive has not yet
experienced that ascetic discipline of mind

known to us as the critique of knowledge. To him the world is a more or less fluid phenomenon within the stream of his own fantasy, where subject and object are undifferentiated and in a state of mutual interpretation. "All that is outside, also is inside," we could say with Goethe. But this "inside," which modern rationalism is so eager to derive from "outside," has an *a priori* structure of its own that antedates all conscious experience. It is quite impossible to conceive how "experience" in the widest sense, or, for that matter, anything psychic, could originate exclusively in the outside world. The psyche is part of the inmost mystery of life, and it has its own peculiar structure and form like every other organism. Whether this psychic structure and its elements, the archetypes, ever "originated" at all is a metaphysical question, and therefore unanswerable. The structure is something given, the precondition that is found to be present in every case.[7]

What is of special interest to our study is not primarily the archetypes, which Jung describes as elements of psychic structure, but the positing of the psyche in its most fundamental condition. Jung wishes to avoid metaphysical questions in regard to the psyche, for he is working primarily with an hypothesis, not a metaphysical entity. In describing the psyche he says:

"The psyche is nothing different from the living being. It is the psychical aspect of the

living being. It is even the psychical aspect of
matter. It is a quality."[8]

For Jung this quality of the living being appears to be developmental, as is evidenced by human progress from lower to higher stages of consciousness. This developmental process is described by Jung in "Psychology of the Child Archetype":

> ...Primitive mentality differs from civilized chiefly in that the conscious mind is far less developed in scope and intensity. Functions such as thinking, willing, etc. are not yet differentiated; they are preconscious, and in the case of thinking, for instance, this shows itself in the circumstance that the primitive does not think *consciously,* but that thoughts *appear.* The primitive cannot assert that he thinks; it is rather that "something thinks in him." The spontaneity of the act of thinking does not lie, causally, in his conscious mind, but in his unconscious. Moreover, he is incapable of any conscious effort of will; he must put himself beforehand into the "mood of willing" or let himself be put—hence his *rites d'entree et de sortie.* His consciousness is menaced by an almighty unconscious; hence his fear of magical influences which may cross his path at any moment; and for this reason, too, he is surrounded by unknown forces and must adjust himself to them as best he can. Owing to the chronic twilight state of his consciousness, it is often next to

impossible to find out whether he merely dreamed something or whether he really experienced it. The spontaneous manifestation of the unconscious and its archetypes intrudes everywhere into his conscious mind, and the mythical world of his ancestors.... It is not the world as we know it that speaks out of his unconscious, but the unknown world of the psyche, of which we know that it mirrors our empirical world only in part, and that, for the other part, it moulds this empirical world in accordance with its own psychic assumptions. The archetype does not proceed from physical facts, but describes how the psyche experiences the physical fact, and in so doing the psyche often behaves so autocratically that it denies tangible reality or makes statements that fly in the face of it.[9]

Jung sees in the process of development of the psyche from unconsciousness to consciousness a fundamental state of psychic tension which must be continually resolved at varied developmental stages. Though consciousness is continually expanded, Jung sees the contents of the unconscious as inexhaustible; hence a constant need for resolution of these two poles of experience. The empirical evidence for such an hypothesis Jung finds in uniting symbols. To these symbols and their possibilities of meaning we can look for the illumination of contemporary epistemological questions.

Uniting symbols, according to Jung, appear in the course of psychic development when the intrapsychic (inner subjective phenomena) is experienced is just as real, just as effective and psychologically true as the outward world of reality. For Jung, the uniting symbol represents a balance between the ego (consciousness) and the unconscious. It represents a primordial image of psychic totality which in the symbol is exhibited in a more or less abstract form as a symmetrical arrangement of parts round a midpoint. Among such symbols are the mandalas which express a unified synthetic view of the psyche. In describing the mandala, Jung says:

> It is a very important archetype. It is the archetype of inner order, and it is always used in that sense, either to make arrangements of the many, many aspects of the universe, a world scheme, or to arrange the complicated aspects of our psyche into a scheme. It expresses the fact that there is a center and a periphery, and it tries to embrace the whole. It is the symbol of wholeness.[10].

These symbols occur among all peoples in all cultures; they are among the oldest symbols of humanity. (For example, they can be found on the walls of Lascaux and other primitive caves.) Jung studied them for fourteen years before venturing to interpret them. These symbols appear in many different forms. When they are depicted in the graphic arts, they all show the same typical arrangements and symmetry of pictorial elements. Their basic design is a circle or square symbolizing wholeness; in all of them the relation to a center is accented. Many have the form of a flower, a cross, or a wheel, with an inclination for the number four. In a mandala from Tantric Buddhism, for example, the center is surrounded by a stylized lotus with eight petals, the background consisting of triangles in four different colors which open into four gates representing

Mandala   Henry Reed

four directions. The graphic representation of the four-armed Sun God is a mandala.

Other less graphic and more ideational mandalas can be found in myths. In the Paradise of Genesis are four rivers flowing out of a single river or spring from the place of pleasure. The Chinese concept of Tao, the union of opposites through a middle path is a mandala. The notion of revolving around oneself in a circular movement belongs to the mandala—for example, the androgynous figure in Plato's Symposium and the symbol of the union of Shiva and Shakti in Hinduism. Broadly speaking, the mandalas as uniting symbols are pictures or pictorial concepts of the primal order of the total psyche. They not only express order; they bring it about. To Jung, these symbols give evidence of humanity's primitive and culturally universal involvement with inner psychic experience. They give evidence of the primitive psychic condition of tension, a tension of inner and outer experieence. This tension is temporarily relieved through the uniting symbols, and from its resolution come humanity's highest creative efforts.

Jung has an explanation for this psychic condition in biological terms. He refers to a distinction between the sympathetic (which we would call the autonomic) nervous system and the cerebrospinal system:

> The unconscious is the psyche that reaches down from the daylight of mentally and morally lucid consciousness into the nervous system that for ages has been known as "sympathetic." This does not govern perception and muscular activity like the cerebrospinal and thus control the environment; but, though functioning without sense organs, it maintains the balance of life and through

the mysterious paths of sympathetic excita-
tion, not only gives us knowledge of the
innermost life of other beings but also has an
inner effect upon them. In this sense it [the
sympathetic nervous system] is an extreme-
ly collective system, the operative basis of all
participation mystique, whereas the cerebrospinal function reaches its high point in
separating off the specific qualities of the
ego, and only apprehends surfaces and ex-
ternals—always through the medium of
space. It [the cerebrospinal system] experiences everything as an outside, whereas the
sympathetic system experiences everything
as an inside.[11]

When Jung speaks here of "knowledge of the innermost life of
other beings" he is not referring to specific knowledge or rational
knowledge (which is the work of the cerebrospinal function) but of
what we might call a kind of feeling knowledge which cannot be
expressed discursively. This distinction of two types of knowing is
not new. According to R.B. Onians, the ancients believed in a water
soul as the source of intuitive thinking and a blood soul as the source
of discursive thinking.[12] Francis Cornford and Ernst Cassirer hold
similar distinctions.[13] Of interest to our topic is not the distinction of
two types of knowledge, nor the knowledge itself, but the ultimate
ground of knowledge, which according to Jung's hypothesis, is a
fundamental state of psychic tension. For Jung, this tension is highly
complex and is far from the simple eros-thanatos tension posited by
Freud. For Jung, this tension involves a polarity, a conflict, a pull in
opposite directions. And the polarity is multiple; hence the four
points of the mandala. This inner tension has its outer physical

counterpart; for example, to achieve physical balance, we locate ourselves in space in terms of up, down, left, and right; or north, south, east, and west.

In our inner conceptual world, however, this tension is often expressed in antinomial terms. Jung holds that in order to express the psychological self conceptuality, we must resort to a transcendental concept expressing the totality of conscious and unconscious contents, and that this totality can only be described in antinomial terms. In characterizing this transcendental situation of the self,[14] Jung uses a formula of a quaternion of opposites: the unitemporal and the eternal, the unique and the universal, the spiritual and the material, good and evil.

This quaternion of opposites which Jung uses to express the psychological self and the conceptualized tension within it can be paralled to Kant's four antinomies of pure reason.[15] Operating within a purely conceptual framework, Kant delineates the antinomies involved in the attempt to form the idea of nature as a whole. According to Kant these antinomies arise because any attempt to formulate a rational cosmology must take into account the entire psychic experience of nature and not simply the empirical experience alone as is done in natural science. From the Jungian point of view, we could say that the conceptualization of humanity's fundamental psychic tension is projected in Kant's theses and antitheses about nature. For example, Kant's first antinomy, the temporality and finitude of the world versus its eternity and infinity, parallels Jung's antinomy, the unitemporality versus the eternity, describing the self. Kant's second antinomy, the divisibility versus the indivisibility of nature, parallels Jung's antinomy of uniqueness versus universality in the concept of the self. Kant's third antinomy is concerned with freedom versus necessity in the laws of nature. Jung's antinomy of good and evil in the concept of the self parallels this antinomy, for without freedom, the moral antinomy of good and evil is questionable. Kant's fourth antinomy concerns an absolutely necessary being in connection with nature versus the lack of it. This parallels Jung's spiritual-material antinomy in the concept of the self, where the spiritual is the absolute dimension of the self corresponding to the necessary absolute being in connection with nature. Kant has no resolution of the antinomies in the idea of nature and preserves the polarity of opposites in the dualism of phenomenon and noumenon of his theory of knowledge. In the conscious and dynamic experience of the self, however, this dualism would defeat psychic wholeness which is the universal endeavor of all humanity, without which human beings would be unable to function. Nevertheless, on the conceptual level this union of opposites can only be thought of as their annihilation. Jung holds that this paradox is characteristic of all transcendental situations since it gives adequate expression to their indescribable nature. In the realm of psychology, Kant recognized this necessity of psychic wholeness, for in the *Critique of Pure Reason* he posited the transcendental unity of apperception, a necessary presuppositon of his whole theory of knowledge. However, Kant's subjective unity is a unity and nothing more, and he avoids the objectification of it as substance. The idea of self in Kant's system is a noumenon, a regulative idea of reason. It is neither a metaphysical entity nor a constitutive idea. In Jung's thought, however, the expression of the self and the cosmos is not confined to the purely conceptual level. It is better manifested in the mandala symbols of all cultures.

In summary, thus far we can say that the Jungian *a priori* involves the positing of a framework of experience which Jung relates to the differentiated brain and to the autonomic and cerebrospinal nervous systems. The necessity of balancing the flood of inner and outer stimuli characterizes the psychic situation of human beings. In the uniting symbols of all cultures Jung sees an expression of moments of resolution of this fundamental state of tension. These

moments of resolution mark human stages of developing consciousness. We have described the uniting symbols in a generic way and
noted their appearance in the pictorial and graphic arts and in
mythological and metaphorical contexts. We have seen how the
Kantian and Jungian antinomies, both of which are bridged by
transcendental situations, express on a highly conceptual level this
same state of psychic tension.

To return now to the epistemological questions raised at the
beginning of this chapter: following Jungian thought, what we take
to be "the given" in the order of knowing can be neither the outer
empirical fact nor the inner subjective state but must be a resolution
of the two, and this resolution will be continually necessary following developing psychic stages. Furthermore, the process is unending
since we are dealing with two open ends: the unfathomable depths of
the unconscious and the unlimited possibilities of human consciousness. Hence, we cannot speak of *the* given but rather of *a* given.

Secondly, in Jungian thinking, the complex symbolism of language and the conceptualized schemes made possible in it, such as,
philosophical categories and their root metaphors, have their origins
in more primitive psychic states. In these states a basic human
tension and its resolutions in terms of developmental archetypal
experiences are expressed in the more primitive symbols of ritual
and myth. Jung says on this point:

> It is impossible to derive any philosophical
> system from the fundamental thoughts of
> primitive man. They provide only antino-
> mies, but it is just these that are the inex-
> haustible source of all spiritual problems in
> all times and in all civilizations.[16]

The works of Cornford and Cassirer complement Jungian
thinking in this regard. For Jung, Cornford, and Cassirer, philoso-

phical speculation does not stop with pragmatic considerations of
"the word" nor with a final reference to subjectivity. All three
philosophers explore a collective subjectivity wherein the word is
seen in the context of human symbolism as a whole. Jung says:

> I am of the opinion that the union of rational
> and irrational truth is to be found not so
> much in art as in the symbol *per se;* for it is
> the essence of the symbol to contain both the
> rational and the irrational. It always expresses
> the one through the other; it comprises both
> without being either.[17]

Finally, in Jungian thinking we could view all systems of
thought including logical systems as vast and intricate symbols of
unity within the linguistic-conceptual realm. The necessity of the
unity of these intricate systems of symbols can be found in their
evidence of internal consistency. In the last analysis, however, symbols of unity must be considered as historical facts, since they can
function dynamically only to the extent that they create order.
Hence uniting symbols as systems of thought must be continually
transcended as human consciousness develops, for the Jungian *a
priori* belongs to process itself and can be understood only in terms of
the historical moments of that process.

28

CHAPTER 2

All references to C. G. Jung's works, unless otherwise indicated, are taken from the *Collected Works* (C. W.) second edition, 20 vols., Princeton University Press.

1. C. I. Lewis, "The Given Element in Empirical Knowledge," *Philosophical Review,* LXI (April 1952); also C. I. Lewis, *Mind and World Order: Outline for a Theory of Knowledge* (New York: Charles Scribner's Sons, 1929); Hans Reichenbach, "Are Phenomenal Reports Absolutely Certain?" *Philosophical Review,* LXI (April 1952); also Hans Reichenbach, *Experience and Prediction* (Chicago: University of Chicago Press, 1952); and Everett W. Hall, *Philosophical Systems: A Categorical Analysis* (Chicago: University of Chicago Press, 1960).

2. Max Black, *Models and Metaphors* (Ithaca: Cornell University Press, 1962).

3. Mikel Dufrenne, *Language and Philosophy* (Bloomington: Indiana University Press, 1963).

4. Immanuel Kant, *Critique of Pure Reason,* trans. Norman Kemp Smith (New York: St. Martin's Press, Inc., 1961), pp. 42-43 (A2; B3).

5. "The Role of the Unconscious" (1918), C. W., 10:10-11 (14).

6. "The Archetypes and the Collective Unconscious" (1934), C. W., 9, i:66 (136).

7. *Ibid.* 101 (187)

8. Richard I. Evans, *Conversations with Carl Jung and Reactions from Ernest Jones* (Princeton: D. Van Nostrand Co., 1964), p. 83.

9. "Psychology of the Child Archetype" (1940), C. W., 9, i:153-154 (260).

10. Evans, *Conversations with Carl Jung,* p.63.

11. "The Archetypes and the Collective Unconscious," *op. cit.,* pp. 19-20 (41).

12. R. B. Onians, *Origins of European Thought about the Body, the Mind, the Soul, the World, Time and Fate* (Cambridge, England, 1954); also Edward G. Ballard, "On Ritual and Persuasion in Plato, " *Southern Journal of Philosophy,* 11 (Summer 1964).

13. Francis Cornford, *From Religion to Philosophy* (New York: Longmans, Green and Co., 1912); also Ernst Cassirer, *Language and Myth,* trans. Susanne K. Langer (New York: Harper and Bros., 1946).

14. "Aion; Researches into the Phenomenology of the Self" (1951), C. W., 9, ii:62-63 (115-116).

15. Kant, *Critique of Pure Reason,* pp. 384-484 (A 406-567; B 432-595).

16. "Archaic Man" (1931), C. W. 10:71 (144).

17. "The Role of the Unconscious," *op. cit.,* p. 18 (24).

Shifting Shapes Fuse Space-Time   Fay Zetlin

CHAPTER 3

THE IMPACT OF HUMAN CONSCIOUSNESS ON THE DYNAMICS OF THE WORLD:

Synchronicity: An Acausal Concept for Contemporary Metaphysics

Substance, time, space, causality are difficult terms for contemporary metaphysicians who in their speculation must confront the relativity principle. Duration, concresence, prehension, actual entity are terms better suited to their purpose. Whitehead's presuppositions that nature is organic and that number lies at the base of the real world are generally conceded. Yet the task of the contemporary metaphysician must go beyond nature and number to the creative involvement of human beings in the world. And here the incommensurability between the outer world of process and the inner world of human subjectivity seems, as Kant has told us, to make the task of metaphysics impossible. The physical sciences with their necessary methods, postulates, and axioms give us one outlook, while the less exact but more individual descriptions of human subjective states reflected in art, myth, and religion give us another view. Is there any grounding for the two, any continuum which can be discovered and described through relevant categories? Is there any structural unity between the so-called "rational" or scientific dimensions of human experience and the "non-rational" feeling/emotive life of human beings? While Whitehead's metaphysics of process provides needed categories, his terms are too general to adequately accommodate the finding of the human sciences.

On the other hand, C.G. Jung, while always claiming that metaphysics was not his task since he was by profession a physician, psychoanalyst and anthropologist, did provide in his extensive writings some useful categories which philosophers may find illuminating. Among these is the concept of synchronicity. Here I take an opposite view to that of one of Jung's biographers, who claims that this concept is "philosophically sterile" because it leads us no further in our thought and understanding. On the contrary, I contend that not only is the concept useful in the philosophy of process by pointing to a bridge between the understanding of nature and the findings of the human sciences, but also it illuminates the understanding of human creativity. In developing this theme, I shall go beyond Jung to the works of some of his interpreters.[1]

At the core of contemporary metaphysics is the relativity principle. In the world view of relativity, the universe is never static because there is always the next increment of consciousnes (in Whitehead's terms "alternate modes of abstraction")[2] and thus the perpetual presence of change in every situation of the universe. Relativity presupposes that the causal explanation of energy transformations is adequate, since the very notion of relativity alters, if not entirely suspends, time and space upon which the causal notion depends. Furthermore, the medium of energy transformation in both the physical and psychic (human) realms is open to speculation. Is the medium a physical continuum or a psychic continuum? Can one be reduced to the other? Or does a third realm ground both the physical and the psychic dimension of reality? If so, how can such a ground of being be understood in terms of relativity? Furthermore, how can the dynamics of individual creative acts including conscious willing and the experience of freedom be accommodated?

Jung confronted these questions in seeking an explanation for the empirical findings involved in the practice of psychotherapy. He and Einstein were associates around the turn of the century when Einstein was working on the relativity concept. At that time, Jung was seeking to develop a concept that would be the equivalent of the relativity theory with the added dimension of the psyche. Thus

Einstein's theory of relativity became the base and starting point for Jung's own thinking about synchronicity.[3]

While the concept of synchronicity originates in the context of Jung's psychological synthesis, it need not be tied to his entire scheme of categories, for the notion can be translated meaningfully into other systems of thought and used fruitfully. Jung used the term to refer to a kind of simultaneity or "meaningful coincidence" of two or more events, where something other than the probability of chance is involved.[4] Such phenomena include the following.

> 1. The coincidence of a psychic state in the observer with a simultaneous, objective, external event that corresponds to the psychic state or connection between the psychic state and the external event, and where, considering the psychic relativity of space and time, such a connection is not even conceivable.
>
> 2. The coincidence of a psychic state with a corresponding (more or less simultaneous) external event taking place outside the observer's field of perception i.e. at a distance, and only verifiable afterward....
>
> 3. The coincidence of a psychic state with a corresponding not yet existent future event that is distant in time and can likewise only be verified afterward.
>
> In groups 2 and 3 the coinciding events are not yet present in the observer's field of perception, but have been anticipated in time in so far as they can only be verified afterward.[5]

The phenomena described above includes situations commonly known as telepathy, precognition, psi-phenomena, and the like. In Jung's view it is not the "perception which is necessarily para or supranormal but the *event itself.*" The event is not "miraculous" but merely "extra-ordinary" and unexpected, and then only from the standpoint which takes causality as axiomatic, while from the statistical standpoint it is simply a matter of random phenomena. Jung believed that "exceptions are just as real as probabilities" and that the "premise of probability simultaneously postulates the existence of the improbable." Consequently, he holds that "it would be advisable to consider Psi-phenomena in the first place as *sua sponte* facts and not as supranormal perceptions."[6] The uncertainity of the relation of these "facts" to time and space does not necessarily depend on a supranormality of our perceptions but rather on the relativity and only partial validity of time and space categories.

In this connection, Jung puts forth an hypothesis of an "acausal connection, i.e., a non-spatial and non-temporal conditioning, of events." He argues that since causality is a statistical truth, exceptions must occur in which time and space appear to be relative; otherwise the truth would not be statistical. He adds that on this epistemological basis "one *must* conclude that the possibility does exist of observing non-spatial and non-temporal events"—the very phenomena which we actually do observe in synchronistic situations contrary to all expectations.[7]

What is significant philosophically is not simply Jung's description of psi-phenomena, however insightful this consideration may be to epistemology, but especially his emphasis on the *unique event* in which the observer participates. Likewise, it is Jung's characterization of the event itself that is relevant to metaphysics.

If indeed an "acausal connection" and a "non-spatial and non-temporal conditioning of events" occurs, then we need further categories to elucidate this situation. Jung posits an *a priori* structure of the psyche which is similiar to the Kantian *a priori* but expanded to include preformed patterns of apperception (archetypes) that are not inherited ideas but inherited universal *possibilities of ideas*.[8] He does not deny a world of objects with which the mind interacts in the order of knowing, but holds, nevertheless, that our very perception is conditioned by the *a priori* structure of the psyche. In Jung's conception, the psyche is not a thing or a metaphysical entity but a *quality* of the living being and in a larger sense the "physical aspect of matter."[9] Matter and psyche appear to be two aspects of the same reality, one quantitative and the other qualitative.

Of the qualitative dimension of psyche, Jung says that it is "not subject to the laws of time and space, as it is on the contrary capable of suppressing them to a certain extent." It is able to manifest timelessness and spacelessness, "eternity" and "ubiquity." This factor Jung calls the archetype, a structural element of the psyche found everywhere and at all times. In it all individual psyches are identical with each other and function as if they were one individual psyche (or collective psyche). Consequently, in psi-phenomena, which points to an essential identity of two separate events (for example, the act of prevision and the objective precognized fact), the factor in question is one and the same inside and outside the individual human psyche. But from the point of view of the collective psyche, there is no "outside." In our ordinary minds we are in the world of time and space and within the separate individual psyche, but from the point of view of the archetype (an autonomous structuring element of the collective psyche), we are in a world-system whose space-time categories are relatively or absolutely abolished.[10]

Regarding space and time, Jung says that he would not go so far as to say that the categories of space and time are definitely non-objective. He would rather ask on which level or in which world space and time are valid. In the three-dimensional world they are certainly and inexorably objective, but he adds, "we have the definite experience that occasionally—presumably under certain conditions—they behave as if they were relatively subjective, that is, relatively non-objective." One is not sure how far the relativity can go. And one does not know whether a level or world exists in which space and time are absolutely abolished, but, Jung concludes, "we remain within the limits of human experience when we accept the fact that it is the psyche which is able to relativize the apparent objectivity of time and space."[11]

In a synchronistic situation (the meaningful coincidence of two or more events in which time and space are relativized) the explanation would be that the autonomous archetype of the collective psyche is manifested. This manifestation occurs in the individual psyche in space and time or in the three-dimensional world, but since the synchronistic situation involves several non-causally related events, these may be known only in a way in which space and time are suspended, such as in cases of precognition or telepathy where no causal elements could be involved. Jung is thus positing a fourth dimension to the psyche, a qualitative element which transcends the time-space limitations of the individual. This dimension can be referred to as "collective" inasmuch as all individuals participate in it. It is also referred to by Jung as "the final view."[12] However, Jung's finality must not be thought of in terms of causality as in the notion of Aristotle's final cause. Instead, finality appears to refer to the order and meaning which the individual can discover in the situation as it relates to one's own life.

Thus we come to the key notion in Jung's concept of synchronicity: inasmuch as a synchronistic situation involves an individual in a meaningful coincidence of events which are non-causally related, only the individual can discover the connection and one cannot do so except in terms of the meaning of one's own life. Thus the bridge between psyche and nature can be made solely by the individual through conscious recognition of the connection and through discovery of the meaning of the connection for oneself, which is also the qualitative dimension of the event. Furthermore, the discovered (or uncovered) meaning can lead to a conscious intervention in process through conscious knowledge and willing and to active participation in the on-going creation through freedom, while on the unconscious level the discovered "meaning" can lead to a change of attitude on the part of the individual, which will affect the whole archetypal process and thereby serve to "constellate" surrounding "events" differently—another aspect of human creativity. Thus the individual is crucial to the structure and order of the universe. Furthermore, from this point of view, the spiritual dimension, the final view, is removed from the fixed (predestined) conception which is necessarily entailed when the understanding of the human psyche is related exclusively to the three-dimensional world.

I have used extraordinary (singular) cognitive instances in order to delineate the characteristics of a synchronistic situation. However, synchronicity is not limited to these situations. Jung says one is "correct in assuming that synchronicity, though in practice a relatively rare phenomenon, is an all-pervading factor or principle in the universe, i.e., in the *unus mundus* [psychophysical universe], where there is no incommensurability between so-called matter and so-called psyche." He adds, "in this connection I have always come upon the enigma of the *natural number*. I have a distinct feeling that number is a key to the mystery, since it is just as much found as it is invented. It is a quality as well as a meaning."[13]

Jung's intuition about number being the key to understanding the mystery of the commensurability of matter and psyche was not fully developed in his lifetime. His followers have taken up the task. What Jung did see was that number has both a quantitative and a qualitative aspect which is simultaneously manifested in the physical world and the psyche. In physics mathematics, or the dimension of quantity, is the ordering principle in the macrocosm, and in

psychology the archetype, or the dimension of quality, is the ordering principle in the microcosm (the human psyche). However, as the
archetype is also an ordering principle rooted in the collective psyche
at the psychoid level (a level beyond the individual psyche) and is
thus a qualitative dimension of matter, the archetype as ordering
principle appears a complement of the quantitative dimension, and
thus the two together present the psychophysical universe from
both sides. Furthermore, since both quantity and quality are aspects
of number, the total experience of number sheds light on the ultimate relationship of matter and psyche, and also points to a third
realm, or continuum, in which this primordial possibility of order
exists. Here we are not far from the intuition of the Pythagoreans
and the notion of the Platonic Forms, with, however, a crucial
difference: namely the dynamic and creative participation of the
individual human psyche in process.

The final point in this presentation of the concept of synchronicity is the understanding of number in the above context. In taking
up this theme, Marie-Louise von Franz[14] holds that in the last
analysis our mental processes are based on numerical structures
which harmonize with the structure of the universe.

All numbers can be viewed as qualitatively differentiated manifestations of the primal one—a mathematical symbol of the *unus
mundus,* isomorphic to the collective psyche—which Dr. von Franz
sees as possessing a relatively homogenous "field" aspect. From the
point of view of the individual psyche, this "numerical field" (in
which individual numbers figure as energic phenomena or rhythmical configurations) is organized around the central archetype of the
Self (experienced as the unity of consciousness in each individual).
The number one is thus the symbolic manifestation of the primordial experience of unity. Two can be seen as the symmetry aspect of
the one-continuum. If this property of the number two is intellectu-
ally hypostatized and confronted with the primal one, the number

three arises out of the confrontation as their synthesis, or as the symmetrical axis in the bipolarity of the one-continuum. According to this view, the three then represents the unitary aspect of the bipolar one-continuum that has become conscious. The intellectual step from two to three is a retrograde one, a reflection leading back to the primal one. This principle can be repeated with all subsequent numbers. The number three taken as a unity related back to the primal one, becomes the fourth. The four is understood not to have originated progressively, but to have retrospectively existed from the very beginning. It is in a sense "found" or "discovered" as are all other numbers.

Dr. von Franz points to this qualitative dimension of number in different cultures. For example, in medieval thinking five is not merely a fifth element added to the four known ones, but represents their realized unity of existence. Similarly, in ancient Chinese thinking, eleven, the number of tao, is not taken in the quantitative sense of ten plus one but signifies the unity of the decade in its wholeness. This aspect of number, because of its retrograde connection to the one-continuum, produces an isomorphism with the timeless primal unity of existence. In terms of synchronicity, therefore, phenomena can appear in the numerically formulated flow of time which produces a sense of temporality in which events can be causally related, but phenomena can also appear in an entire "bundled" pattern which produces a timeless constancy of meaning or the sense of an eternal presense of a single act.

In the behavior of archetypal dynamics (and hence in synchronistic phenomena) the archetypes seem to manifest themselves in "ordered sequences" of which the number series forms the most primitive expression, while the ordered sequences also exist simultaneously and timelessly in the one-continuum. Because this ordering factor manifests itself in a psychic as well as a physical energic phenomenon, Dr. von Franz concludes that we are dealing with one and the same energy which we designate as physical energy when it is physically measurable or as psychic energy when it become psychically and introspectively perceptible. Psychic energy is experienced as "intensity" or as varying gradations of feeling or emotion which point to a latent physical energy in psychic phenomenon. Hence the psyche should be capable of appearing in the form of mass in motion, while matter should possess a latent psychic aspect insofar as psychological interaction takes place. Number appears bound up with the latent material aspect of the psyche and with the latent psychic aspect of matter.

Jung points to the fact that all emotional and therefore energy-laden psychic processes evince a striking tendency to become rhythmical. Any kind of excitement displays a tendency to rhythmical expression, perservation, and repetition, which would explain the basis of social rhythmical and ritual activities practiced by primitives. Through rhythmn, psychic energy and the ideas and activities bound up with it are imprinted and firmly organized in consciousness. Dr. von Franz sees the application of rhythm to psychic energy as perhaps the first step toward cultural formation and hence toward spiritualization. She points to the fact that the ancient Chinese conception of number is based on association with this type of rhythmical activity and that number is utilized to assess feeling-intensities of all things that produce a psychic effect. Moreover, numbers represent all the rhythmical configurations of the universe in its wholeness. This aspect of number is experienced as retrogressively brought back into relation with the primal unity as meaning, for the uniting characteristic of meaning can draw the broadest categories of phenomena together into a *Gestalt*. In the spiritual and mental realms of the psyche, quantitative universal numbers are demultiplied and drawn back again into their unified forms. This *Gestalt*, however, is bound up with meaning.

Jung says that meaning, compared with life, appears to be the younger event, while the reverse is actually the case because the forms which are used for assigning meaning are historical categories reaching back into the mists of time. These forms structure the emotional intensities underlying human feeling life, and they are also manifested in the symbolic structures of human culture. These historical categories (or archetypes somewhat analogous to the Platonic realm of eternal ideas) are not equivalent to meaning, but they are, nevertheless, the *a priori* condition for the possibility of finding meaning in life.

Therefore, while the possibilities of meaning are *a priori* to human consciousness, the discovery of meaning can only be made by the individual. The ability of the human psyche to interact in process in the temporal world and at the same time to experience the world retrogressively, that is, to spontaneously order events to the one-continuum bringing them into relation with the primal unity as meaning, seems to be rooted in the ultimate order of the universe. This order is cognitively experienced through the quantitative dimension of number underlying the scientific knowledge of the world, while the order is qualitatively experienced through the feeling and emotional intensities of the human psyche. The coming together of these two dimensions of human experience as manifested in synchronistic phenomena involves the individual in the universe as both participant and interpreter.

In summary, the concept of synchronicity is relevant to contemporary metaphysics because it sheds light on the ultimate ground of the order of the universe in which the individual participates (1) through one's scientific understanding of the world and (2) through one's feeling/emotional life. Both of these dimensions of human experience can be viewed as manifestations of the primal order of the universe revealed through the quantitative and qualitative aspects of number. As Dr. von Franz has pointed out, the emotional structures, which in the last analysis lie at the root of all qualitative experience, reach consciousness through varying intensities or innate repetitive cycles of behavior. The rhythms through which these cycles are experienced and related to the primal unity of consciousness can be regarded as a kind of qualitative "counting," not unlike the quantitative "measuring" relative to any particular empirical perspective.

In a synchronistic situation, the individual experiences the order of the universe on both quantitative (causally ordered) and qualitative (emotionally intensified) levels. Hence, the coming together of events constituting a "meaningful coincidence" (which only the individul can discern, since one's own individual emotional life is involved) reveals a unique situation in which the order of the psyche and the order of the cosmos coincide. The concept of synchronicity is, therefore, a key to the understanding of the mysterious interaction of matter and psyche, the ultimate order in which matter and psyche are grounded, and the dynamic process in which the individual creatively and reflectively participates.

43

CHAPTER 3

All references to C. G. Jung's works, unless otherwise indicated, are taken from the *Collected Works* (C.W.) second edition, 20 vols., Princeton University Press.

1. Ira Progoff, *Jung, Synchronicity and Human Destiny: Noncausal Dimensions of Human Experience* (New York: The Julian Press, 1973) and Marie-Louise von Franz, *Number and Time: Reflections Leading toward a Unification of Depth Psychology and Physics,* trans. Andrea Dykes (Evanston, Ill.: Northwestern University Press, 1974).

2. Alfred N. Whitehead, *Science and the Modern World* (New York: The Free Press, 1967), p. 118.

3. Progoff, *Jung, Synchronicity and Human Destiny.*

4. "Synchronicity: An Acausal Connecting Principle (1955) C. W. 8:520 (969).

5. *Ibid.* 526 (984-985).

6. *C. G. Jung Letters,* ed. G. Adler and A.Jaffé, trans R. F. C. Hull, Bollingen Series XCV:2 (Princeton: Princeton University Press), vol. 2, p. 542.

7. *Ibid.* 539-40.

8. See chapter 2.

9. Richard I. Evans, *Conversations with Carl Jung and Reactions from Ernest Jones* (Princeton: D. Van Nostrand Co., 1964), p. 83; also, "On-the Nature of the Psyche" (1947) C. W., 8:215 (418).

10. *Letters,* 399.

11. *Ibid.* 398.

12. "On Psychic Energy" (1928), C. W. 8:4-6 (3-5).

13. *Letters,* 400; also "On the Nature of the Psyche" (1947) C. W. 8:215 (418).

14. Marie-Louise von Franz, *Number and Time.*

CHAPTER 4

HUMAN CREATIVITY IN ART AND LIFE:

C.G. Jung's Philosophy of Creativity

Underlying C.G. Jung's psychological explanation of creativity is a view of humanity, nature, and the cosmos. For Jung, creativity is at once an instinct rooted in the human organism and at the same time a cosmic process having an autonomy of its own which Jung identified as spirit. Spirit makes an individual creative, even taking possession of one's life and robbing one of freedom in order that works of culture may be born. But spirit also works cooperatively with a conscious and willing individual opening the way to atemporal dimensions of knowledge and freedom. The aim of this chapter is to set forth the essential categories which Jung employs in describing creativity both as a dynamic human process and as a principle *sui generis* encompassing and structuring an individual and the world. In developing this topic, concepts have been taken freely from Jung's works, and categories have been interpreted in the broader theme of creativity.

While Jung always claimed he was not a metaphysician and wanted to maintain an empirical stance in his work, his categories not only took him beyond the domain of science, they clearly placed him in a transcendent perspective. For example, wishing to keep psychology rooted in an empirical foundation, he listed creativity as an impulse or instinct along with four other instincts: hunger, sexuality, the drive to activity, and reflection.[1] He regarded all instincts as impulses which carry out actions from necessity without conscious motivation, and he saw them as inherited rather than individually acquired. In regard to creativity, however, Jung expanded the notion of instinct, pointing out that while instinct in general denotes a system of stably organized patterns and tends toward unlimited repetition, the individual has the distinctive power of creating something new in the real sense of the word. Hence, he saw the creative impulse as similar in nature and as having a close connection to instincts yet distinct from any one of them.[2]

Moving beyond the purely biological realm, Jung noted that the question of instinct cannot be dealt with psychologically without considering the archetypes. This category refers to what Jung considered to be the *a priori* forms of intuition found in the deeper strata of the unconscious. He saw instincts and archetypes as compelling the individual to specifically human modes of existence and specifically human patterns of perception and apprehension.[3] The archetype or psychic dynamic of the creative process Jung called spirit.[4] We see then, that while Jung's philosophy of creativity has an empirical base in the biological realm, namely, instinct, it also implies a spiritual dimension. These two aspects of human activity come together in what Jung termed the unconscious, which he understood as the source or ground of universal ordering principles.[5]

In Jung's general philosophy, all processes, both human and cosmic, are united in the collective unconscious. Consciousness, on the other hand, Jung defines as an inward perception of the objective life process. Similarly, he describes archetype as an instinct's perception of itself.[6] In Jung's system, archetypes function as primordial structuring principles of human and cosmic life and also as agencies through which the life process can become conscious. However, for Jung archetypes as primordial structuring patterns remain universal. Only their concrete manifestation through the creation of human symbols permits them to reach consciousness. Thus, conscious human life is a symbolic life. Human creative instinct, transformed by the power of the creative spirit makes human culture and human consciousness possible.[7]

In Jung's concept of creativity, an individual participates in the objective life process in two ways: (1) one may be simply used in the process, that is, one's very being may become the soil out of which works of culture are generated, and (2) through consciousness and freedom, one may intervene in the creative process and dynamically affect it. In the first case, an individual often becomes the mere instrument of the creative archetype. Jung says that such a person is wholly at one with the creative process and may become so identified with the work that one's intentions and faculties are indistinguishable from the act of creation itself.

Jung speaks of the compelling nature which the creative principle sometimes manifests. Of the works of art which result, he says,

> They come as it were fully arrayed into the world, as Pallas Athene sprang from the head of Zeus. These works positively force themselves upon the author; his hand is seized, his pen writes things that his mind contemplates in amazement. The work brings with it its own form; anything he wants to add is rejected, and what he himself would like to reject is thrust back at him. While his conscious mind stands amazed and empty before this phenomenon, he is overwhelmed by a flood of thoughts and images which he never intended to create and which his own will could never have brought into being.[8]

Jung says that in such situations the artist experiences creativity as an apparently alien inner impulse which must be followed and obeyed. Although this power cannot be commanded, it is one's own nature revealing itself. Nevertheless, the artist realizes no identity with the creative process and is subordinate to the work standing outside it as a second person.

In this sense, Jung refers to the creative process "as a living thing implanted in the human psyche." It lives and grows in an individual like a tree in the earth from which it draws nourishment. He says, "The unborn work in the psyche of the artist is a force of nature that achieves its end either with tyrannical might or with the subtle cunning of nature herself, quite regardless of the personal fate of the man who is its vehicle."[9] The true work of art which results is something supra-personal which soars beyond the personal concerns of its creator and cannot be judged by personal criteria.

In terms of Jung's philosophy of creativity as a whole, we may say that Jung posits a force, both instinctual and spiritual, which transcends a person's ordinary nature and uses the individual as an instrument for its own ends. This creative principle, call it archetype or spirit, belongs to an order of reality in which an individual can participate but over which one can have little control. Jung's thought thus far implies a metaphysics of process in which the artist becomes the instrument of a transcendent power.

However, we said earlier that Jung also sees an individual as participating in the objective life process with consciousness and freedom. Can one then intervene in the process and dynamically affect it. Not all creativity is the result of magical states of possession. A person can cooperate with the creative process particularly in terms of the individual's own life. In order to develop this aspect of creativity, we are in need of another of Jung's categories to further our understanding, namely the soul.

Jung speaks of the soul as a function of relation between the subject and the inaccessible depths of the unconscious. As a creative function, the soul gives birth in symbolic form to images which from the rational standpoint of consciousness may be worthless because they cannot be immediately turned to account in the objective world. However, they can be utilized eventually in artistic, philosophic, and religious endeavors, or else squandered.[10]

In Jung's system, the soul acts as mediator between the collective unconscious and conscious ego life. Through its several functions (intuitive, thinking, sensing, and feeling)[11] the soul is able to balance the ego personality with the objective life process and specifically with the self, the unknown dimension of the individual. The cooperation of the conscious ego with this wider self is the task of individuation, which is also a creative process. For Jung, individuation and creativity go together.[12]

The images which the soul presents to consciousness through dreams, intuitions, hunches, synchronistic phenonema, fantasies, etc. are merely raw material for the creative endeavor of individuation. These images have to be worked on, put in a form, and developed into a process for differentiating the personality.[13] A human life from this point of view is like a work of art (a metaphor which may not be alive to many people). Yet, according to Jung, the creative instinct is in everyone. He asks, "...what can a man 'create' if he doesn't happen to be a poet?" And he answers, "...if you have nothing at all to create, then perhaps you create yourself."[14] In another context, he comments, "...we must not forget that...very few people are artists in life; that the art of life is the most distinguished and rarest of all the arts. Who ever succeeded in draining the whole cup with grace?"[15]

How then does the creative principle function in the art of life? First, we must take note of the images which the soul presents to consciousness. The essence of these images is their spontaneity, their primary "givenness." Jung says, "I am indeed convinced that creative imagination is the only primordial phenomenon accessible to us, the real Ground of the Psyche, the only immediate reality."[16] He speaks of the image-creating mind as the matrix of all those patterns that give apperception its peculiar character[17] and refers to the primordial images as "being in the soul." Jung says, "...this is the only form of being we can experience directly; all other realities are derived from and indirectly revealed by it."[18]

The ground of these images found in dreams, fantasies, intuitions, synchronistic phenomena, etc. is the unconscious, the matrix mind which has the quality of creativeness attached to it. Jung likens this concept to the Eastern notion of the Universal Mind which is without form, yet is the source of all forms.[19] He says that insofar as the patterns or forms of the unconscious belong to no time in particular, seeming eternal, they convey a peculiar feeling of timelessness when consciously realized.

Images reach consciousness through affect, that is, through energy charged in an archetypal process. Affect is that which at any given moment in an individual life represents the natural urge of life.[20] The orchestration of diverse archetypal functions experienced as affects is involved in normal living, and the harmonious accommodation of all of these processes is a state of wholeness. Jung sees the archetypal process as both within and without the individual; thus when an outer conflict is constellated in one's life, an inner process occurs as well, and vice versa. He says,

> Under normal conditions, every conflict stimulates the mind to activity for the purpose of creating a satisfactory solution...The suspension thus created 'constellates' the unconscious—in other words, the conscious suspense produces a new compensatory reaction in the unconscious. This reaction (usually manifested in dreams) is brought to conscious realization in its turn. The conscious mind is thus confronted with a new aspect of the psyche, which arouses a different problem or modifies an old one in an unexpected way. The procedure is continued until the original

conflict is satisfactorily resolved. The whole process is called the "transcendent function." It is a process and method at the same time. The production of unconscious compensations is a spontaneous *process;* the conscious realization is a *method.* The function is called "transcendent" because it facilitates the transition from one psychic condition to another by means of the mutual confrontation of opposites.[21]

In this description, a mediation between inner images and outer situations is made possible through a principle which Jung calls the "transcendent function." He says the process is spontaneous, and the conscious realization of it reveals a method of bringing opposites into harmony.

Jung holds that everyone must possess the possibility of a higher level of development which could come about under favorable circumstances. He observed in people who did develop that the new impetus usually came from an obscure possibility either outside or inside themselves which they accepted and with which they grew. For some the new thing came from outside, and for others inside, but never exclusively either from within or without. He said, "If it came from outside, it became a profound inner experience; if it came from inside, it became an outer happening. In no case was it conjured into existence intentionally or by conscious willing, but rather seemed to born along on the stream of time."[22] Jung asks, "What did these people do in order to bring about the development that set them free? As far as I could see they did nothing...but let things happen."[23] This is the Taoist idea of action through non-action. The ability to let things happen in the psyche is an art which few people practice because consciousness is always interfering by helping, correcting, and negating, never leaving the psychic processes to grow in peace. Jung speaks of the necessity of relaxing the "cramp in the conscious mind" and permitting the emergence of a new attitude which admits the irrational and the incomprehensible. Thus the flow of life through inner images and outer events can go forth. However, he pointed to the necessity of retaining the previous values if they be genuine so that one does not swing too far to the other side, slipping into unfitness, unadaptedness, or even insanity. Jung sees the individual as a self-regulating system in whom a necessary polarity remains. This polarity is mediated by the transcendent function,[24] which is another dimension of the archetype of creativity or the spirit. Through this principle the individual maintains contact with the deeper ground of one's being.

For some, the creative process flows with an easy grace, at least for a while. But the demands of life usually call for higher levels of consciousness and more refined degrees of moral participation. In this connection, Jung speaks of two requisites: the first is a method and the second a moral condition.

A technique which Jung suggests for understanding spontaneous images is the hermeneutic method. Through this technique images and symbols can act as signposts, providing the clues the individual needs in order to carry on one's life in harmony with oneself. The hermeneutic method is a technique used in Jungian analysis, but it is not confined to pathological situations. Jung refers to it as "an art, a technique, a science of psychological life, which the patient, when cured, should continue to practice for his own good and for the good of those amongst whom he lives."[25] Jung describes the method in this way:

> The essence of hermeneutics...consists in
> adding further analogies to the one already
> supplied by the symbol: in the first place

> subjective analogies produced at random...then objective analogies provided...out of general knowledge. This procedure widens and enriches the initial symbol, and the final outcome is an infinitely complex and variegated picture of elements of which can be reduced to their respective *tertia comparationis*. Certain lines of psychological development then stand out that are at once individual and collective... Their validity is proved by their intense value of life.[26]

Through this treatment of images and fantasies, an individual can synthesize one's conscious life with the deeper roots of the psyche, but then, Jung says, a moral requirement presents itself. The moment one maps out a line of advance that is symbolically indicated, a person must take the way of the individual lifeline recognized as one's own and continue along it until such time as an unmistakable reaction from the unconscious reveals that one is on the wrong track. Jung says, "He who does not possess this moral function, this loyalty to himself, will never get rid of his neurosis. But he who has this capacity will certainly find the way to cure himself." He adds, "Infallibly, in the last resort, it is the moral factor that decides between health and sickness."[27]

The construction of "lifelines" reveals to consciousness the ever-changing direction of the currents of libido. The lifeline constructed by the hermeneutic method is temporary, for life does not follow straight lines whose direction can be predicted far in advance. Instead, the lifelines are points of view and attitudes that have a provisional value. When there is a decline in vital intensity, a noticeable loss of libido, or an upsurge of feeling, the moment indicates that one line has been quitted and a new line begins or ought to begin. In terms of psychotherapy, Jung says, "...the true end of analysis is reached when the patient has gained an adequate knowledge of methods by which he can maintain contact with the unconscious and has acquired a psychological understanding sufficient for him to discern the direction of his lifeline at the moment."[28]

To recapitulate: we have seen earlier that Jung's philosophy of creativity implies a metaphysics of process in which the artist in the creation of works of culture becomes the instrument of a transcendent power. We see now that the creative spirit as both imagination and transcendent function guides and structures an individual life. We see further that a person can consciously cooperate with the creative principle in one's own life through reflection upon the images given and through moral integrity and courage to follow one's individual path. Thus far we have been discussing images given in a moment of time and having reference to events in a familiar space-time world. Yet some experiences are inexplicable in the familiar world, experiences involving images and psychic states which, because of their numinosity, call for further amplification and added categories of thought.

We have said that spontaneous images come from the unconscious, which Jung describes as the matrix mind having the quality of creativeness attached to it. Jung's complex concept of the unconscious is a key to his entire system. The notion "unconscious" presumes a quality of becoming conscious. Since this quality in Jung's system is attached to all reality, even at the "psychoid"[29] level, meaning that which is beyond human consciousness, Jung seems to be postulating in all pervasive system. From the human standpoint, the concept of soul is necessary since it refers to the relation between the individual and the unconscious. Through soul (or psyche) the structures of the unconscious even at the psychoid level can ultimately be manifested in concrete symbolic form.

However, in Jung's conception, the psyche or soul is not a thing or a metaphysical entity, but a quality of the living being and in a larger sense the "physical aspect of matter."[30] Thus the soul as a function or quality in the individual is continuous with the quality of all reality. While the soul as conscious mind functions in the world of space and time, the soul as unconscious mind, both personal and collective, has access to images which are atemporal, images of the future as well as the past. The archetypes or primordial forms of the unconscious can structure the images of the soul so as to manifest timelessnes and spacelessness, "eternity" and "ubiquity." From this point of view, spontaneous images are both inside and outside the individual psyche. Jung says, "In our ordinary minds we are in the worlds of time and space and within the separate individual psyche. In the state of the archetype we are in the collective psyche, in a world-system whose space-time categories are relatively or absolutely abolished."[31]

What we have been describing applies to situations involving a spontaneous presentation of inner images and outer events in what Jung calls synchronistic phenomena: situations commonly known as telepathy, precognition, psi-phenomena, and the like. In these cases, one or more inner images or psychic states correspond with external events in such a way that the categories of space, time, and causality must be abolished. A connection is felt among these images and events, an experience of meaningful relatedness, but with no rational explanation in terms of linear thinking and space-time categories. In Jung's conception, the underlying connection of these images and events can be attributed to an archetype manifested symbolically in profound and compellling ways in terms of crises or fundamental changes in one's life.[32] We are reminded that repetition and rhythm are means by which activities reach consciousness in the first place; thus, when an individual is bombarded by images and events somehow related yet defying space-time descriptions, the necessity to take cognizance of the phenomena is all the more reinforced. Consequently, synchronistic situations are especially in need of hermeneutic treatment and moral seriousness in the process of individuation or the truly creative life. Furthermore, since these situations take one out of space and time for the moment and thereby permit one to participate in the larger dynamics of process, the creative potential of the individual is all the more enhanced. One can then respond creatively through conscious reflection, through the ability to change attitudes, and through freedom to act. At such times one may experience most forcibly the power of the creative spirit.

Let us sum up the general categories of Jung's philosophy of creativity. Creativity is rooted in human and cosmic life as a fundamental principle referred to as instinct/archetype/spirit. This principle has its foundation in the collective unconscious, which transcends the purely human sphere to include ultimately the psychoid or non-human levels of reality. The collective unconscious is seen as the qualitative dimension of the one reality with which an individual comes in contact through soul, a concept which for Jung implies the principle of relation between the individual and the unconscious. The soul presents images to consciousness through the transforming power of the archetype of creativity, which Jung calls spirit. Spirit sometimes uses artists against their will in the creation of works of culture taking possession of their lives and robbing them of freedom. However, an individual through consciousness and moral integrity can cooperate with spirit, particularly in the creation of one's own life. In this latter process, Jung suggests the Taoist art of letting things happen (both inner image and outer events), the hermeneutic method of amplification of symbols, and the recognition of the transcendent function through which images and events are brought into harmony. This dynamic process helps to release through affect the lifelines of the individual. A new situation then emerges which demands of the individual integrity and courage to pursue one's own path. An individual can now experience genuine creative freedom manifested in changes of inner attitudes as much as in outer courses of action. For Jung, the inner situation helps to constellate the outer and vice versa, since the archetypes which structure the upsurge of life are manifested both within and without the individual. Synchronistic phenomena are dramatic manifestations of this inner and outer connectedness. In these situations one transcends the normal three-dimensional mode of being in the world to participate briefly in the *mundus archetypus*.[33] The genuine artist through the images of the soul is in touch with the deeper structures of the collective unconscious and through creative efforts manifests these structures in symbolic form in a work of art in the space-time world. The genuine artist of human living likewise is able to touch deeper levels of the unconscious. Through diffuse awareness of images which the soul presents, through willingness to let things happen, through openness to hermeneutic explorations of inner images and outer events, and finally through moral integrity and courage, a truly creative person is able to cooperate with the spirit in making one's own life a work of art.

58

CHAPTER 4

All references to C. G. Jung's works, unless otherwise indicated, are taken from the *Collected Works* (C. W.) second edition, 20 vols., Princeton University Press.

1. "Psychological Factors in Human Behaviour" (1936) C. W., 8:118 (245).

2. *Ibid.*

3. "Instinct and the Unconscious" (1919) C. W., 8:129-138 (263-282).

4. "The Phenomenology of the Spirit in Fairytales" (1948) C. W., 9, 1:212-213 (393).

5. "On the Nature of the Psyche" (1947) C. W., 8:159-234 (343-442).

6. "Instinct and the Unconscious" *op. cit.* 136-137 (277).

7. "The Structure of the Psyche" (1927) C. W., 8:158 (342).

8. "On the Relation of Analytical Psychology to Poetry" (1923) C. W., 15:73 (110).

9. *Ibid.* 75 (115).

10. "The Type Problem in Poetry" (1921) C. W., 6:250-252 (425-426).

11. "General Description of the Types" (1921) C. W., 6:330-495 (556-857).

12. "The Development of Personality" (1939) C. W., 17:167-186 (284-323).

13. "The Type Problem in Poetry" *op. cit.* 252 (427).

14. "Foreword to Suzuki's 'Introduction to Zen Buddhism' " (1939) C. W., 11:556-557 (906).

15. "The Stages of Life" (1933) C. W., 8:400 (789)

16. *C. G. Jung Letters,* ed. G. Adler and A. Jaffé, trans. R. F. C. Hull, Bollingen Series XCV:1 (Princeton: Princeton University Press), vol. 1, p. 60.

17. "Psychological Commentary on 'The Tibetan Book of the Great Liberation' " (1939) C. W., 11:490 (781).

18. *Letters* vol. 1, p. 60.

19. "Psychological Commentary on 'Tibetan Book of the Great Liberation' " *op. cit* 490 (782).

20. The term "affect" is used frequently in Jung's writings. For a precise definition, see "General Description of the Types" *op. cit.* 411-412 (681).

21. "Psychological Commentary on 'The Tibetan Book of the Great Liberation' " *op. cit.* 489 (780).

22. "Commentary on 'The Secret of the Golden Flower' " (1931) C. W., 13:16 (18).

23. *Ibid.* 16 (20).

24. "The Psychology of the Unconscious" (1943) C. W., 7:110 (186); also, "The Relations Between the Ego and the Unconscious" (1938) C. W., 7:219 (358-359).

25. "The Structure of the Unconscious" (1947) C. W., 7:295 (502).

26. *Ibid.* 291 (493).

27. *Ibid.* 293-294 (498-499).

28. *Ibid.* 294 (501).

29. "The Conjunction" in *Mysterium Coniunctionis* (1954) C. W., 14:551 (788); also, "On the Nature of the Psyche" *op. cit.* 215-216 (419-420).

30. Richard I. Evans, *Conversations with Carl Jung and Reactions from Ernest Jones* (Princeton: D. Van Nostrand Co., 1964) 83; also, "On the Nature of the Psyche" *op. ct.* 215 (418).

31. *C. G. Jung Letters,* ed. G. Adler and A. Jaffé, trans. R. F. C. Bollingen Series XCV:2 (Princeton: Princeton University Press), vol. 2, p. 399.

32. "Synchronicity: An Acausal Connecting Principle" (1952) C. W., 8:419-531 (816-977).

33. "On the Nature of the Psyche" *op. cit.* 198 (394); also, "Mysterium Coniunctionis", C. W., 14:534 (761).

CHAPTER 5

HUMAN LIFE AS CONSCIOUSNESS AND MORAL ACTION:

Imagination and Life

This chapter is a sequel to the previous chapter in which I analyzed the role of the creative principle, the Spirit, in visionary art and in the creative life. In this chapter, I hope to give further development to the topic of individuation, amplifying the metaphor of a human life as a work of art, more specifically as an on-going creation. I shall focus on the dynamic interaction of inner images and outer events and note the crucial importance of recognizing and accommodating the creative element of moral experience. My concern is the dynamically lived human life in the stream of process. The seminal ideas for this chapter are found in Jung's writings.

Jung says the essence of the creative imagination is to provide something new in the real sense of the word.[1] The willingness of an individual to accept this dimension of oneself requires a more advanced stage of development of both personal consciousness and moral integrity. At this level, one is not seeking simply to balance the four functions of one's psychic life in the Jungian sense; instead, the individual has already achieved a limited experience of this balance and is able to live creatively in the world. In this context, preoccupation with images of the soul involves more than adjusting, complementing, making harmony, and discovering meaning. The images can now be seen in relation to the ongoing creation of one's own life and the world. Myths of creation from this perspective become living metaphors, for life itself is then experienced as an ongoing creation.

When one takes the images of the soul in process which is open-ended in terms of the beginning and end of the present conscious world and also in terms of all possible worlds, a new dynamics emerges. In this context, images need not point exclusively to one's eventual future or even death. Images can be freed from all immediate associations and collective conceptions and can be opened up to the absolutely unknown and unimaginable. Only then is the full creative potentiality of the image possible. As long as images are seen in the context of the known, namely, the present categories of thought and analogues of feeling of the individual or even in relation to collective symbols, images are somehow "reduced" and likewise limited. To temporarily forego all such associations is to free images completely and to open them to still wider perspectives to the unknown. What I am suggesting ties in with Jung's admonition to take every dream in its uniqueness and to put aside all previous conceptions when approaching it.

The disengaging of the conscious attitude with its corresponding focus permits the true logic of the imagination to assert itself. By logic of the imagination, I mean the process of genuine analogy, which is the spontaneous creation of image upon image that the unconscious provides to the truly open mind and heart. This experience is both an intellectual and a moral or feeling approach to images. Jung tells us that the numinosity of images is manifested in both their clarity and emotional tone. This gripping of both mind and heart is evidence, according to Jung, of the grounding of images in the archetypes which structure the life process. The individual who is in touch with one's diverse psychic functions in the Jungian sense is able to experience both inner images and outer events in multidimensional spheres reflecting one's many-faceted psychic capabilities. This individual in good psychological health often experiences the conscious and unconscious dynamics of one's life as moving on parallel lines. For this person, synchronicity is an ordinary fact of experience. For this person also, the unconscious sometimes takes an active role in the process of differentiation. Jung says,

The reaction of the unconscious is far from

being merely passive; it takes the initiative
in a creative way, and sometimes its purpo-
sive activity predominates over its custom-
ary reactivity. As a partner in the process of
conscious differentation, it does not act as a
mere opponent, for the revelation of its contents enriches consciousness and assists
differentiation.[2]

Jung reminds us that images are found not only in dreams but
in all symbols. He says,

Symbols, like dreams, are natural products,
but they do not occur only in dreams. They
can appear in any number of psychic manifestations: there are symbolic thoughts and
feelings, symbolic acts and situations, and it
often looks as if not only the unconscious but
even inanimate objects were concurring in
the arrangement of symbolic patterns.[3]

The individual whose mind and heart is willing to accept
images wherever one finds them—in both dreams and waking fantasies, in outer events and unexpected happenings, in nature and
concrete objects, in social relationships and personal encounters—in
a word, in one's entire phenomenal world—this individual finds rich
resources all around oneself for both creativity and spiritual growth.
I would describe the above psychological attitude as a conscious
engagement in or return to what Jung has called "participation
mystique"—that primitive mental state of no differentiation between
inner subjective experiences and outer events. In our usual habit of
mind, however, Jung says we have learned to discard the trimming

of fantasy and have thus lost a quality that is still characteristic of the primitive mind.

> Primitive thinking sees its object surrounded by a fringe of associations which have become more or less unconscious in civilized man. Thus animals, plants, and inanimate objects can acquire properties that are most unexpected to the white man....What we call psychic identity or *participation mystique* has been stripped off our world of things. It is exactly this halo, or "fringe of consciousness," as William James calls it, which gives a colourful and fantastic aspect to the primitive world. We have lost it to such a degree that we do not recognize it when we meet it again, and are baffled by its incomprehensibility. With us such things are kept below the threshold; and when they occasionally reappear, we are convinced that something is wrong.
> ....We are so used to the rational surface of our world that we cannot imagine anything untoward happening within the confines of common sense. If our mind once in a while does something thoroughly unexpected, we are terrified and immediately think of a pathological disturbance, whereas primitive man would think of fetishes, spirits, or gods but would never doubt his sanity.[4]

The questions we raise are these: Is it possible to return to a primitive mode of perception? Is it desirable? Surely creative artists do so for inspiration in their work. The creative individual functioning within the diverse dimensions of psychic life should be able to do so also. If one's life is integrated, one is not forced to live exclusively in the rational mode, or solely in the emotional realm, nor would one be given over entirely to the passions of the body or to the inspirations of the spirit. One would have reached a stage which spiritual writers characterize as the highest level of development; namely, the spontaneous and free engagement in the life process, the tao, the uninhibited, selfless, yet total surrender to the dynamics of the moment.

So much emphasis in Jungian thought has been given the discovery of meaning, the role of the archetypes, the work of the gods, and so forth, that a more passive and Apollinian emphasis has developed in Jungian psychology as a whole. One may acknowledge the realm of the gods, but as long as one is in the land of the living one is not permitted to dwell too exclusively in the divine sphere. Life is essentially dynamic. The gods live through human beings; without human life the gods become empty symbols. To live a too symbolic life, a life apart from the full engagement of the body in all of its dimensions in process, is to aspire to the realm of the gods and to commit the sin of hubris, for which in all mythologies a human being is repeatedly punished. Herculean ego effort, however, is not the only alternative. Somewhere between the two extremes lies the path.

Jung warned against a too symbolic life in which emotional powers or "numinosities" of the archetypes are brushed aside or repressed. In referring to those who admit of the existence of the archetypes, but then treat them as if they were mere images and forget that they are living entities that make up a great part of the human psyche, he says,

> As soon as the interpreter strips them of
> their numinosity, they lose their life and

become mere words. It is then easy enough
to link them together with other mythological representations, and so the process of
limitless substitution begins; one glides from
archetype to archetype, everything means
everything, and one has reduced the whole
process to absurdity. All the corpses in the
world are chemically identical, but living
individuals are not. It is true that the forms
of archetypes are to a considerable extent
interchangeable, but their numinosity is and
remains a fact. It represents the *value* of an
archetypal event. This emotional value must
be kept in mind and allowed for throughout
the whole intellectual process of interpretation. The risk of losing it is great, because
thinking...abolishes feeling values and vice
versa.[5]

Jung is saying that emotional values must be preserved because
they are evidence of the numinosity, of the power of the archetype.
Archetypes not only structure the world; they bind human beings to
it compelling them through instinct and passion to participate in
process. Of the necessity of active engagement in life for the individual who wants to know the human psyche, Jung says,

He would be...advised to...wander with human
heart through the world. There, in the horrors
of prisons, lunatic asylums and hospitals, in
drab suburban pubs, in brothels and gamb-
ling-hells, in the salons of the elegant, the
Stock Exchanges, Socialist meetings, chur-

ches, revivalist gatherings and ecstatic sects,
through love and hate, through the experience of passion in every form in his own
body, he would reap richer stores of knowledge than text-books a foot thick could give
him...[61]

Wisdom comes not through a controlled engagement in life, not
from a Herculean effort to structure life from an ego standpoint, but
through a willingness to freely give oneself up to life in all of its
dimensions. Images of the soul carry with them a numinosity, an
emotional tone which binds human beings to the land of the living.
The gods as gods are dead; they live only through individuals
through their willing or unwilling participation in the ongoing
creation.

To be a victim of the gods (or fate) in the active engagement in
life is one thing; to cooperate with them is another. The creative
individual in touch with the gods through an habitual recognition of
their presence revealed through the synchronistic concurrence of
inner images and outer events lives freely in the world bound neither
by literalism nor by images hypostasized through aesthetics or
intellectualism. What makes the difference, what goes beyond these
lifeless extremes, what constitutes the crucial element of the creative life, is passion, involvement, and connection through the
emotions.

In this context, Jung contrasts the more passive oriental spirituality to his own view:

The Indian's goal is not moral perfection, but
the condition of *nirdvandva*. He wishes to
free himself from nature; in keeping with
this aim, he seeks in meditation the condition of imagelessness and emptiness. I, on

the other hand, wish to persist in the state of lively contemplation of nature and of the psychic images. I want to be freed neither from human beings, nor from myself, nor from nature; for all these appear to me the greatest of miracles. Nature, the psyche, and life appear to me like divinity unfolded—and what more could I wish for? To me the supreme meaning of Being can consist only in the fact that it is, not that it is not or is no longer.

....I cannot be liberated from anything that I do not possess, have not done or experienced. Real liberation becomes possible for me only when I have done all that I was able to do, when I have completely devoted myself to a thing and participated in it to the utmost. If I withdraw from participation, I am virtually amputating the corresponding part of my psyche. Naturally, there may be good reasons for not immersing myself in a given experience. But then I am forced to confess my inability, and must know that I may have neglected to do something of vital importance....

A man who has not passed through the inferno of his passions has not overcome them. They then dwell in the house next door, and at any moment a flame may dart out and set fire to his own house. Whenever we give up, leave behind, and forget too much, there is always the danger that the

things we have neglected will return with
added force.[7]

I suggest, following these words from "Memories, Dreams,
Reflections," an important difference between Jung's ideal and that
presented in archetypal psychology, in James Hillman, "The Dream
and the Underworld,"[8] and Roberts Avens, "Imagination is Reality."[9] Both of these tests emphasize the imaginal realm as imaginal,
as opposed to literalism. I suggest a third stance, a mediation in
which the imaginal and life flow together in the physical world, in
the body, where the two, the imaginal and the concrete, move on
parallel lines reflecting each other synchronistically in the creative
life. This occurs in those individuals who, moving beyond the mere
necessity to balance the diverse facets of psychic life, and having
already achieved a degree of balance, can now consciously and freely
give themselves over to the dynamics of existence. Roberts Avens
quoting D.T. Suzuki on Zen Buddhism expressed a similar goal. Yet
the Buddhist ideal emphasizes "the effortless and desireless life of
stillness in the midst of the most intense comings and goings of all
things," and in this ideal seems a passivity, an egolessness, inimical
to the Jungian ideal and to Western consciousness generally. I say
this particularly in reference to Jung's stance on the relationship of
consciousness to morality and to his insistence that the individual
has a duty to be conscious and moral. We might call morality a
Western invention, since Eastern spirituality as Jung says, transcends the moral problem. I would like now to amplify the relevance
of the moral question to the creative life.

Exactly what does Jung mean by morality? Surely he did not
mean the unquestioned following of a set of moral rules nor the blind
acceptance of social conventions. On the contrary, he is interested in
the serious consideration of every difficult moral situation in its
context of socially acceptable moral rules vis-à-vis the grounding of
these rules in innate moral consciousness.

The question that concerns Jung is not so much the existence of moral laws, but the origin of these laws and the possible deviation from them, which he attributes to the "original behavior of the psyche." He delineates this question in "A Psychological View of Conscience":

> In practice it is indeed very difficult to dis-
> tinguish conscience from traditional moral
> precepts. For this reason it is often thought
> that conscience is nothing more than the
> suggestive effect of these moral precepts,
> and that it would not exist if no moral laws
> had been invented. But the phenomenon we
> call "conscience" is found at every level of
> human culture.[10]

Conscience, he says, is experienced as an "inner reproach" or a "twinge of conscience," both being a deviation from an inveterate habit or generally accepted rule, a deviation which produces something like shock. This emotional response accompanying moral reactions exemplifies to Jung the original behavior of the psyche. Again it is emotion which registers the connection between the individual and the deeper ground of one's being, emotion felt when conflict occurs between the individual conscience and accepted modes of behavior.

In the creative life, moral considerations are facts of experience, for the individual who is immersed in process cannot escape the accepted precepts of society. Yet for this individual the solution to moral conflicts sometimes does not come from simply following accepted rules, but rather from a deeper ground manifested as a "inner voice." Jung spells out this situation in detail.

It will then be decided which is the stronger:

tradition and conventional morality, or conscience. Am I to tell the truth and thereby involve a fellow human being in catastrophe, or should I tell a lie in order to save a human life? In such dilemmas we are certainly not obeying our conscience if we stick obstinately and in all circumstances to the commandment: Thou shall not lie. We have merely observed the moral code. But if we obey the judgment of conscience, we stand alone and have harkened to a subjective voice, not knowing what the motives are on which it rests. No one can guarantee that he has only noble motives. We know—some of us—far too much about ourselves to pretend that we are one hundred per cent good and not egotists to the marrow. Always behind what we imagine are our best deeds stands the devil, patting us paternally on the shoulder and whispering, "Well done."[11]

Jung asks,

Where does the true and authentic conscience, which rises above the moral code and refuses to submit to its dictates, gets its justification from? What gives it the courage to assume that it is not a false conscience, a self deception?

In answer, he quotes John (I John 4:11) "Try the spirits whether they be of God?" and he states,

Since olden times conscience has been understood by many people less as a psychic function than as a divine intervention; indeed its
dictates were regarded as...the voice of God.
This view shows what value and signficance
were, and still are, attached to the phenomenon of conscience....The question of
"truth,"....as to whether it has been proved
that God himself speaks to us with the voice
of conscience, has nothing to do with the
psychological problem. The *vox Dei* is an
assertion and opinion, like the assertion that
there is such a thing as conscience at all....It
is a *psychological truth* that the opinion exists
that the voice of conscience is the voice of
God.[12]

Jung concludes that anyone who allows conscience this status
should, for better or worse, put one's trust in divine guidance and
follow one's conscience rather than give heed to conventional morality. He holds that conscience, no matter on what it is based, com-
mands the individual to obey the inner voice even at the risk of going
astray. He says,

We can refuse to obey this command by an
appeal to the moral code and the moral views
on which it is founded, though with an
uncomfortable feeling of having been disloyal.
One may think what one likes about an
ethos, yet an ethos is and remains an inner
voice, injury to which is no joke and can
sometimes have very serious psychic consequences.[13]

In moral dilemmas, then, the creative potentiality of an individual is most seriously challenged and the role of the transcendent
function most needed. Jung believes that scarcely any other psychic
phenomenon shows the polarity of the psyche in a clearer light than
conscience. He refers to conscience as an undoubted dynamism, an
energy whose potentiality is based on opposites. Conscience brings
these opposites to conscious perception, and the solution to the
conflict has to come from the creative archetype, the Spirit. He says,
"If one is sufficiently conscientious the conflict is endured to the end,
and a creative solution emerges which is produced by the constellated archetype and possesses that compelling authority, not
unjustly characterized as the voice of God. The nature of the solution
is in accord with the deepest foundations of the personality as well as
with its wholeness."[14]

We may question why Western consciousness is bothered by
moral problems which can be transcended by the Eastern mind. The
answer may lie in the type of differentiation of consciousness which
has evolved in Western culture, a differentiation which Jung's psychology and specifically his concept of individuation attempt to
explain.

The highest levels of Eastern and Western consciousness may
indeed merge in a mutual acceptance of the tao of human existence,
but the two cultures arrive at this higher dimension by different
routes. The Western mind has to deal with the moral problem; the
question is, why? Jung offers an answer in "The Psychology of the
Transference" when he speaks of the two essential elements of
individuation. Individuation, he says,

> ...has two principal aspects: in the first place
> it is an internal and subjective process of
> integration, and in the second it is an equally
> indispensable process of objective relation-

> ship. Neither can exist without the other, although sometimes the one and sometimes the other predominates.[15]

Objective relationships have a psychological counterpart within the individual; but without the outer situation, the inner polarities and the resolutions cannot reach consciousness. Jung says,

> ...the conscious achievement of inner unity clings to human relationships as to an indispensable condition, for without the conscious acknowledgment and acceptance of our fellowship with those around us there can be no synthesis of personality. That mysterious something in which the inner union takes place is nothing personal, has nothing to do with the ego, is in fact superior to the ego because, as the self, it is the synthesis of the ego and the suprapersonal unconscious. The inner consolidation of the individual is not just the hardness of collective man on a higher plane, in the form of spiritual aloofness and inaccessibility; it emphatically includes our fellow man.[16]

The moral problem is inextricably tied up with human relationships and with the foundation of relationships in instinct, in what Jung calls the "kinship libido" which includes the incest taboo and the tension of other conflicting instinctual demands. Social structures today are such that "everyone is now a stranger among strangers," but the kinship libido is still a vital need.

> Kinship libido—which could still engender a
> satisfying feeling of belonging together, as
> for instance in the early Christian commun-
> ities—has long been deprived of its object.
> But, being an instinct, it is not to be satisfied
> by any mere substitute such as creed, party,
> nation, or state. It wants the *human* connec-
> tion. That is the core of the whole transfer-
> ence phenomenon, and it is impossible to
> argue it away, because relationship to the
> self is at once relationship to our fellow
> man...[17]

Relationship to others, or kinship libido, is not only a vital personal
need; it is also the foundation of morality. Jung sees the bond
established by the transference, however hard to bear and however
incomprehensible it may seem, as vitally important not only for the
individual but also for society and for the moral and spiritual progress of humanity.

In "The Psychology of the Transference" Jung is concerned
with the doctor-patient relationship, but the situation is the same in
any relationship in which one person becomes the bearer of another's soul image. Jung delineates the same problem of projections in
his work "Marriage as a Psychological Relationship."[18] In human
relationships, then, with all of their intricate and conflicting instinctual demands, the moral problem is engendered. Relationships are
necessary for the differentiation of consciousness, but they also
make possible the moral and spiritual progress of humanity.

In Western consciousness, the Christian myth of love and
union is one of the basic archetypes of human relatedness. This
archetype carries a whole constellation of psychological situations
within relationships, such as, the vulnerability of infancy, the inno-

cence and trust of childhood, the openness and adventurous spirit of youth, the spiritual marriage, self-surrender, and sacrifice. The Western mind has this special spiritual heritage and its attendant moral problems of concern, responsibility, freedom, and guilt. That mind cannot find its roots only among the pagan gods. It must also include the Christian images in its pantheon.

The work that lies ahead for individuals chosen by the creative spirit to be bearers of truth in the Westernworld is the synthesis of the Christian ideal of human relatedness with the deeper archetypal foundations manifested by the ancient gods. How this work is to be accomplished is the inner secret that lies at the core of every personality engaged in the task. By holding on to the magic thread of imagination, by seeing through literalisms to discover the synchronicity of the moment, by admitting the reality and power of emotions, and by listening to the inner voice, an individual can learn to participate actively, freely, and with full confidence in the ongoing creation.

CHAPTER 5

All references to C. G. Jung's works, unless otherwise indicated, are taken from the *Collected Works* (C. W.) second edition, 20 vols., Princeton University Press.

1. "Psychological Factors in Human Behavior" (1936) C. W., 8:118 (245).

2. "Foreward to Newmann: 'Depth Psychology and a New Ethic' " (1949, 1969) C. W., 18:621 (1418).

3. "Symbols and the Interpretation of Dreams" (1961) C. W., 18:211 (480).

4. *Ibid.* 204-205 (465-466).

5. *Ibid.* 260 (596).

6. "New Paths in Psychology" (1917) C. W., 7:247 (409).

7. C. G. Jung, *Memories, Dreams, Reflections* (New York): Vintage Books, 1961), 276-277.

8. James Hillman, *The Dream and the Underworld* (New York: Harper and Row, 1979).

9. Robert Avens, *Imagination is Reality* (Irving, Texas: Spring Publications, 1980).

10. "A Psychological View of Conscience" (1958) C. W., 10: 443 (836).

11. *Ibid.* 444 (837).

12. *Ibid.* 444-445 (838-839).

13. *Ibid.* 445 (841).

14. *Ibid.* 454-455 (856).

15. "The Psychology of the Transference" (1946) C. W., 16: 234 (448).

16. *Ibid.* 233 (444).

17. *Ibid.* 233-234 (445).

18. "Marriage as a Psychological Relationship" (1925) C. W., 17: 189-201 (324-345).

CHAPTER 6

THE PROBLEM OF EVIL:

Jung and Plotinus on Evil

For both Plotinus and C.G. Jung, the question "Whence Evil?" goes beyond the immediacy of human affairs. Both sages find it necessary to account for evil in a wider metaphysical structure in which God or the One is of crucial importance. Both thinkers are steeped in a mystic or religious tradition in which, partly because of the times in which they lived, the moral problem and the question of ultimate value, namely, the good, is a central issue. Both philosophers find categories for their systems of ideas in Gnostic teaching, though neither sees himself as identified with this dualistic tradition. Both thinkers engage in the polemics of their day in defending their own intuitive visions vis-à-vis the more popular views of their times: Plotinus maintains the unity of the One against Gnostic plurality, while Jung finds in this very plurality a defense for his numinous God images. Finally, while both sages have a private mysticism as a starting point for their basic metaphysical assumptions, both see themselves as participants in a collective wisdom or world soul which transcends their very essence. Yet, for all their similarities, these two philosophers coming from different periods of history separated by over sixteen centuries, have different answers to the question of evil. But just how great is the difference?

For Plotinus, mystic, and beloved teacher of the classic writings of Greek philosophy, especially those of Plato and Aristotle, evil is identified with matter, the final link in a chain of realities beginning with the One. The One is absolutely simple, beyond possibility and actuality, beyond any possible differentiation, for it thinks not, is unconditionally free in its absolute necessity, forever willing itself, unshakable, ever perfect and good in the absolute sense.

The One willing itself is its own revelation and ever producing itself is the Divine Mind or Nous. Nous ever spending the creative force of the One gives rise to the Divine Soul, the principle of motion. Looking back to the pure actuality of Nous, the Divine Soul receives the ideas thereof and after this primordial image she (as Plotinus personifies it) actuates forming the void matter. Thus the Universal Soul is extended into a twofold direction; in respective contemplation toward the higher, she is Psyche in the pregnant sense; as forming power irristibly moving toward the potentially lower, she is Physis, productive Soul. From the Psyche the Gods emanate; from the Physis the daimons. Thus Plotinian theology interpreted popular religions. Ever moving on through countless individuations, the Universal Soul expresses its effluescence in the individual Soul, her miniature issue. The psyche in the individual soul turns to the heights (Nous and the One) while the physis in it acts toward matter, the last step downward.

Remotest from the One, matter is thus the remotest from the Good, and is therefore Evil or the absence of all good. Evil can only be known in relation to Good because one principle unites all things. In the First *Ennead,* Book 8, Plotinus asks, "For what is evil to the soul?" He answers, "It is being in contact with inferior nature; otherwise the soul would not have any appetite, pain, or fear....It is only because of the nature and power of the Good that evil does not remain pure evil."[1] Evil, which consists in the absence of all good, cannot be described as a form. Evil in itself is matter which is the subject of figure, form, determination, and limitation; owing its ornaments to others, it has nothing good in itself.[2]

The irrational part of the soul, then, harbors all that constitutes evil: namely, indetermination, excess, and need. The soul is neither independent of matter, nor by herself perverse. By virtue of her union with the body, which is material, she is mingled with indetermination and is obscured by the darkness with which matter surrounds her. The soul is inclined toward matter because it fixes her glance not on essence but on simple generation whose principle is matter. Since it is the privation of good, matter contains none of it and assimilates to itself all that touches it. The soul already contains matter because she looks at darkness.[3] Matter is thus the final link in the chain of realities, and matter is evil. Yet the soul has an affinity for matter because of its need for generation.

Plotinus' metaphysics has been described as an indivisible synthesis of ontology and ethics.[4] By identifying the One exclusively with the Good, Plotinus could not include matter and evil as necessary principles. Although he borrowed images from the Gnostics of his day in delineating his mythology, in the Second *Ennead,* Book 9, he protested as irrational the Gnostics introduction of a second soul, presumably an evil soul, which they put together from the elements. Against their view, he maintained that the phenomenal world is not an original principle, and consequently matter in the phenomenal world is not primal. He held that the Gnostics are wrong to separate matter in order to account for evil, for no need exists for this.[5] Since Soul itself is the cause of decline or darkness, the world or matter cannot be. The phenomenon of evil can be justified in a world which is essentially of good origin because the One had to be expressed in gradations of every possible kind. Individual objects or events may be bad, but within the total panorama their place can be seen within a necessary good order. The dark is necessary for the light to shine.

While the One is identified with the Good, and while the Divine Mind or Nous as the revelation of the One is also good, only after the emanation of the Divine Soul, the principle of motion, does the void matter enter the metaphysical system. When the Divine Soul actuates, matter enters. The actuality, the productivity, the creativity, necessitates matter and evil. Plotinus says the soul already contains matter because she looks at darkness. The mystery of evil, then, lies in the soul, in the creative powers of the soul. The soul must look at darkness in order for the One to be expressed in gradations of every possible kind. This expression of gradations or differentiation (in Jungian terms "consciousness") is not possible without darkness, without both light and dark, without both good and evil.

Darkness suggests what is not seen, or not yet seen in relation to what is seen already or can be seen in the light (in Jungian terms, the light of consciousness). In the creative process, in order for more of the One to be revealed through the actuality, the activity, of the soul, the One must already have been concealed through the darkness, the potentiality, the evil of the soul.

From a Jungian perspective, this darkness in relation to the soul represents the shadow, both the individual shadow and the collective shadow. This shadow side of reality makes possible the ongoing creation both in the individual and in collective humanity, for Jung approaches the question of creation, matter, and evil from an anthropomorphic standpoint, and through the study of human beings Jung's metaphysical principles of good and evil emerge.

Within the inheritance of Christian neo-Platonism, C.G. Jung's approach to evil stems from the confrontation of his personal psychology with the religious tradition in which he was reared. In "Memories, Dreams, Reflections," he tells us that as a youth he sought in vain from his teachers and from his father who was a clergyman, answers to Christian theological questions, such as: "...if God is the highest good, why is the world, His creation, so imperfect, so corrupt, so pitiable?"[6] What are the reasons for suffering, imperfection, and evil? There were no answers. Later on, through Goethe's Mephistopheles, Jung saw evil as a universal power playing a mysterious role in delivering human beings from darkness and suffering. At the same time, however, the reality of God was for Jung, as he said, "the most certain and immediate of experiences," and he came to realize that the light and darkness of God were facts that could be understood even though they oppressed his feelings.[7] These realizations came to him through reflection upon his inner experiences, his dreams and visions.

However, as a physician and empirical psychologist, and as a witness to the devastating effects of two world wars, Jung was well aware of the reality of evil in human beings and in the world. Hence for him the inadequacy of the Christian doctrine of evil as *privatio boni* wherein evil is a mere diminuation of good and thus deprived of substance. This sense of inadequacy led Jung beyond the Church Fathers to the Gnostics whose arguments were very much influenced by psychic experience.[8]

For the Gnostics, the good, perfect, spiritual God is opposed by an imperfect, vain, ignorant, and incompetent demiurge who later becomes the devil who has created the world. Jung saw the continuation of Gnostic philosophy in alchemy where the dark side is expressed in the conception of Mercurius as the partly material, partly immaterial spirit that penetrates and sustains all things from stones and metals to the highest living organisms. "In the form of a snake he dwells inside the earth, has a body, and spirit, was believed to have a human shape...and was regarded as the chthonic God."[9]

Because Jung approached the reality of God from the psychological side and saw images of God in all cultures as projections of the higher Self, these negative images in Gnosticism and alchemy, he regarded as projections of the "shadow," by which he meant the inferior personality, whose lowest level is indistinguishable from the instinctuality of an animal. Jung says,

> Since the shadow, in itself, is unconscious
> for most people, the snake would correspond
> to what is totally unconscious and incapable
> of becoming conscious, but which, as the
> collective unconscious and as instinct, seems
> to possess a peculiar wisdom of its own and a

> knowledge that is often felt to be super-
> natural. This is the treasure which the
> snake (or dragon) guards, and also the rea-
> son why the snake signifies evil and dark-
> ness on the one hand and wisdom on the
> other. Its unrelatedness, coldness, and dan-
> gerousness express the instinctuality that
> with ruthless cruelty rides roughshod over
> all moral and any other human wishes and
> considerations....[10]

For Jung, these negative images can be seen as the complement to the highest and most positive images of the Self.

In the dualism of the Gnostics, then, Jung found a counterpart to the primordial psychological situation:

> ...the dualism of the Gnostic systems make
> sense, because they at least try to do justice
> to the real meaning of evil. They have also
> done us the supreme service of having gone
> very thoroughly into the question of where
> evil comes from. Biblical tradition leaves us
> very much in the dark on this point, and it is
> only too obvious why the old theologians
> were in no particular hurry to enlighten us.
> In a monotheist religion everything that goes
> against God can only be traced back to God
> himself.[11]

Jung's own philosophy, however, has no difficulty in tracing evil back to God. Evil is a manifestation of the dark side of God. For Jung's God, like Plotinus' One is unconscious, "for it thinks not," but unlike Plotinus' One, Jung's God is not good simply, but is amoral. One must remember, however, that theoretically Jung always approached God from the psychological side.

He said:

> What God is in himself nobody knows; at least I don't. Thus it is beyond the reach of man to make valid statements about the divine nature. If we disregard the shortcomings of the human mind in assuming a knowledge about God, which we cannot have, we simply get ourselves into most appalling contradictions and in trying to extricate ourselves from them we use awful syllogisms, like the *privatio boni*. Moreover our superstitious belief in the power of the word is a serious obstacle to our thinking.[12]

Nevertheless, despite these reservations regarding talk about God, Jung found it necessary for personal reasons in one of his last works, "Answer to Job," to elaborate his own myth about God and man, good and evil. Borrowing concepts from Gnosticism, he delineated a metaphysics in which God, as an amoral masculine being out of touch with his primordial feminine wisdom Sophia, who was with him at the dawn of creation, acts in his unconsciousness in a cold, ruthless, and vengeful ways toward his bride Israel. Job is a case in point. As the innocent victim of injustice and because of this the bearer of a higher consciousness, Job does not retaliate with blasphemy, but humbly searches his soul and accepts the reality of his condition. Job is a witness to the dark side of God.[13]

Unlike Plotinus' One, Jung's God is involved in the dynamics of his creation, and the divine drama is thereby affected. Through human beings, God becomes conscious and moral. Through an individual, God regains access to his unconscious wisdom, Sophia. God's coming to consciousness, like an individual's is an ongoing process. Evil, then is a reality. It does not stem from human beings but from the divine nature itself, which apart from interaction in the human world remains unconscious and amoral. Jung says, "Evil, like good, belongs to the category of human values...."[14] Therefore, from Jung's standpoint, the image of God dynamically effects these values in human creation to the degree that human beings consciously assimilate them.

Although Plotinus and Jung place evil in different metaphysical systems, from a human perspective one could say they agree on several points. For both, evil can be comprehended only in relation to the good. For both, evil is associated with a darkness which permits light and differentiation. For both, this differentiation is possible because of a creative principle associated with Soul, which is both individual and collective. For both, the creative principle associated with Soul brings about a revelation of the one or God through the dynamics of evil or indeterminacy. Finally, for both, evil and indeterminacy can lead the individual through painful differentiation to unity and the Good.

Before concluding, let us consider the metaphysical systems of each philosopher. A metaphysics is a philosopher's rational ordering of an intuitive grasp of "what is." The intuition is first, and the logic or rational "talk" which the philosopher uses to conceptualize the vision is second. One could say that Jung and Plotinus had similar visions of "what is." Both were mystics, and both were absorbed with a sense of the absolute in relation to good and evil and in relation to human beings. But their philosophical approaches are different. In the metaphysics of the Greeks who looked outward, Plotinus ordered his vision accordingly and placed the absolute, the One, in an objective system of reality. For Plotinus, no separation or distance occurs between the conceptual scheme and the reality which it explains. The explanation *is* the reality, though Plotinus, like Plato, sees the phenomenal world as a lesser reality. On the other hand, Jung, a follower of Kant who had conducted the Copernican Revolution in the realm of ideas, approached "what is" from the subjective standpoint. That is why Jung's mystical grasp of the absolute is referred to as the "God-image" and not God. Jung does not always adhere closely to these distinctions in his writings and his discourse often slips from one realm to the other; nevertheless, I think that Jung wanted always to maintain the subjective standpoint. That is why he called his philosophy "his myth." Consequently, "Answer to Job" must be seen in this light, as Jung's myth about God, humanity, good, and evil.

Granted that the metaphysics of the two philosophers can be separated by the contemporary subtleties of sign theory and philosophical analysis, striking similarities remain in the two systems. Actually, Jung's metaphysics (which he never set forth in a systematic way, as he always maintained that his categories were clumsy) rests upon a hypothetical unity which he calls the *unus mundus*.[15] In the *unus mundus* (the unitary world), psyche (soul) and physis (matter) are one. The archetypes, primordial ordering principles, are rooted in the *unus mundus* and manifest themselves in both the physical and psychic realms. Jung's principle of synchronicity rests upon this intuition. Furthermore, Jung's concept of the collective unconscious carries with it the implication that all reality is potentially conscious. Through human beings consciousness of the collective unconscious can come about. The soul, which includes the world soul and individual human souls, represents the collective unconscious in the process of becoming conscious. The God-image is a human projection of the ultimate possibilities of this process as the higher Self, as well as the limit of human finiteness, a limit necessary for inner integrity.

If we look at these metaphysical concepts in relation to Plotinian categories, we find many similarities. The One of Plotinus and the *unus mundus* of Jung both share the same ineffable unknowable realm. The Nous of Plotinus and the archetypes of Jung likewise point to a similar intuition concerning the primordial order of "what is." The universal soul of Plotinus and the world soul of Jung, both of which involve the dynamics of creation, matter, form, and good and evil, also suggest a similar intuition of reality as process. And in both philosophical schemes evil is accounted for at this third level, namely, the realm of Soul. In the realm of Soul, Jung's God-image is a projection of the archetype of the Self and like all archetypes is paradoxical; it has both positive and negative aspects. Hence, the God-image as anthropomorphic has both good and evil qualities. What Jung's own private mystic experience of the absolute was, we shall never know. As he said, "What God is in himself nobody knows; at least I don't." The question is, did Jung really see evil in the absolute, or did he see evil only in the human relation to the absolute, that is, in the God-image? Jung was very much steeped in the Christian tradition. He may not have agreed with the old theologians who accounted for evil as *privatio boni,* he may have accounted for evil in the psychological and religious sense as the dark or shadow side of both human beings and God and thus removed the total blame for evil from conscious individuals; nevertheless, the absolute of his metaphysical system, as the hypothetical *unus mundus,* is beyond good and evil. From this perspective, little difference appears between the intuitions of Jung and Plotinus about reality and the nature of evil.

CHAPTER 6

All references to C. G. Jung's works, unless otherwise indicated, are taken from the *Collected Works* (C. W.) second edition, 20 vols., Princeton University Press.

1. Plotinus, First *Ennead,* Book Eight; "Of the Nature and Origin of Evils," B, 15. Plotinus, *Complete Works,* 4 Vols., ed. by Kenneth Sylvan Guthrie, (Comparative Literature Press, 1918), Vol. IV, p. 1163.

2. *Ibid.* A, 3, p. 1146.

3. *Ibid.* A, 4, p. 1148.

4. John M. Rist, "Plotinus on Matter and Evil," *Phronesis* 6 (1961), 154-66, p. 160.

5. Plotinus, Second *Ennead,* Book Nine; "Against the Gnostics; or, That the Creator and the World are Not Evil." Plotinus, *Complete Works, op. cit.,* Vol. 3, pp. 599-639.

6. *Memories, Dreams, Reflections* (New York: Vintage Books, 1963), p. 59.

7. *Ibid.* p. 63.

8. "Aion: Researches into the Phenomenology of the Self" (1950), C. W., 9, ii:41-42 (74-75).

9. *Ibid.* 231-232 (366-367).

10. *Ibid.* 234 (370).

11. "A Psychological Approach to the Trinity" (1948) C. W., 11:169 (249).

12. "Jung and Religious Belief" (1958), C. W., 18:710 (1595).

13. "Answer to Job" (1954) C. W., 11:359-470 (553-758).

14. "Aion: Researches into the Phenomenology of the Self" *op. cit.,* 47 (84).

15. "Flying Saucers: A Modern Myth" (1959), C. W. 10:409-412 (778-780); also "Mysterium Coniunctionis" (1954) C. W., 14:462-466 (660-664); 476 (679); 533-543 (759-775).

CHAPTER 7

THE ROOTS OF SYMBOLIC FORMS:

Structures in Art Media*

The problem of structural relations among art media needs to be reinvestigated in the light of contemporary theories. In an aesthetics which is rooted in classical metaphysics, the problem of structural relations among the arts can be explored in a larger theory of being with its essential structures. In an aesthetic theory which does not rely on an ontology, either classical or contemporary, the problem of structural relations among art media is more complex. The purpose of this chapter is to investigate the problem in the light of Susanne Langer's *Mind: An Essay of Human Feeling,* Marshall McLuhan's theory of media, and C. G. Jung's theory of the collective unconscious. The goal is to offer insight toward a theoretical basis for the study of structural relations among the arts.

Taking the work of art as art symbol, we can say with Langer that works of art are images of the forms of feeling which are always organic or "living." Feeling is taken as a heightened form of life. The art symbol is thus a symbolic projection of how vital and emotional and intellectual tensions appear, i.e., how they feel. Langer makes feeling the starting point of a philosophy of mind. She holds, however, that there is no basic vocabulary of lines and colors and elementary tonal structures or poetic phrases, with conventional emotive meanings, from which complex expressive forms, works of art, can be composed by rules of manipulation. Instead, the work of art is primary. One might call it a "metaphorical symbol." It is not a

*First published in *Tulane Studies in Philosophy: Aesthetics* I, XIX, 1970.

simple metaphor, but a highly elaborate one in which the elements of composition are articulated to different degrees. The elements mean one thing in one of their internal relations and something else in another. For Langer the essential structural elements of all the arts, considered here as projected images of feeling, consist in the establishment and organization of tensions:

> The most fundamental elements seem to be tensions; and upon closer inspection, tensions show some peculiarly interesting traits. By their very occurrence they immediately engender a structure. They act on each other in a great variety of ways—they can be handled so as to intersect without losing their identity, or contrariwise, so that they fuse and compose entirely new elements. They can be intensified or muted, resolved either by being spent or by being counterbalanced, modified by a touch and all the while they make for structure. This appears to be true in all the great orders of art; in every one of them, a general range of tensions is set up by the first element—line, gesture or tone— which the artist establishes. In performed works this immediate effect of a single, first presented element is often apparent to the audience as well as to the author.[1]

In considering the basic structural elements of all the arts as consisting in the organization of tensions, in Langer's theory one always encounters the structure in a medium. A primary question of this chapter now emerges: can the structures encountered in one art medium be related or transformed to the structures of another medium? Langer holds that no parallel elements among the arts correspond in any regular fashion because the structure of a work of art is nothing as simple as an arrangement of given elements by a series of combinatory operations. Futhermore, the problem of determining the equivalents which elements in one domain of sense have in some other domain is a psychological one, properly undertaken in psychology laboratories. Although the investigation of sensory parallels carried on for several decades has yielded stock examples, Langer holds that the results of controlled experiment have not provided any usable parallels for a more scientific construction of, for example, "color organs" or "tone poems." Nevertheless, she believes that "some significant relationships certainly exist between data of different sensory orders"[2] and that relations exist among the arts "even such as rest ultimately on sensuous equivalences,"[3] but she does not think relations exist of whole categories of sensations to other whole categories, permitting systematic substitutions. She feels that a better approach to the problem is to determine what different sensations have an emotive character in common and then to determine how artists exploit this fact.

Hence, the problem of structural relations among art media needs to be examined at another level, a generic level, rather than at the level of one medium to another. Returning to Langer's thesis that the structures of the arts consist in the organizations of tensions, or "virtual tensions spanning tensions," and that the art symbol as living form is a projected image of feeling or felt life, let us examine (1) the media in which we find art symbols, and (2) the ground of the art symbol, namely human feeling life, to continue our investigation of the central problem.

We turn now to McLuhan's ideas concerning media in general. McLuhan views all media as human extensions and holds that no medium has its meaning or existence alone, but only in constant interplay with other media. Media, being extensions of ourselves, depend upon us for their interplay and their evolution. McLuhan holds that while people become fascinated by an extension of themselves in any material other than themselves, they also become numbed by this extension. Consequently, in the dynamics of process, media interact among themselves. The moment of the meeting of media is a moment of freedom and release from the ordinary trance and numbness imposed on them by our senses. Thus, all media function as active metaphors in their power to translate experience into new forms. McLahan's ideas are illuminating to the question of the evolution of art forms. He cites Cubism as an example of one medium giving way to another: "Cubism, by giving the inside and outside, the top, bottom, back, and front and the rest, in two dimensions, drops the illusion of perspective in favor of instant sensory awareness of the whole."[4] When specialized segments of attention shift to the total field, the medium becomes the message. The message is not what the medium is about, but the medium itself, that is, the structure and configuration of the whole. However, in any medium or structure a "break boundary" occurs at which the system suddenly changes into another or passes some point of no return in its dynamic processes. One of the most common causes of breaks in any system is the cross-fertilization with another system.

McLuhan's ideas concur with Langer's in the sense that in the work of art no "content" is to be translated from one medium to another. For McLuhan the message is confined to the medium, to this medium here and now. Furthermore, McLuhan holds that electric technology, the medium of the modern age, has eliminated time and space factors in human association and created involvement in depth. By imposing unvisualizable relationships that are the result of instant speed, electric technology dethrones the visual sense and forces us to the synthesis and close interaction of sense. The electronic environment is turning the world into a "global village"; it is "re-tribalizing" humanity. The ultimate conflict between sight and sound, between written and oral kinds of perception, between "hot" linear, visual perception and "cool" intergrational perception is upon us. The new electric technology extends the human nervous system "in a global embrace"; it "points the way to an extension of the process of consciousness itself, on a world scale, and without any verbalization whatever."[5] McLuhan sees electric technology as achieving "the consciousness of the unconsciousness." This consciousness, McLuhan describes as "an inclusive process which does not postulate content, as a post-linguistic "comprehension" of the universe. Viewing the history of culture as explosion away from—and implosive return to—tribal conditions, McLuhan compares modern society to a primitive tribal society that "lives mythically and in depth." He defines myth as "the instant vision of a complex process that ordinarily extends over a long-period."[6]

Whether we accept McLuhan's thesis about media and the modern age, his central thought does support the point of view of this chapter: that structural relations among media, if any exist, are better studied at the level of the symbolic process in general. In other words, we might look to the phenomena of human beings continually extending themselves in media and thereby continually altering their views of the world and their relationship to it for further light on the question. McLuhan himself has expressed a faith in the "ultimate harmony of all being."[7]

This leads to the second point of investigation of our problem: the ground of the art symbol or human feeling life. McLuhan's concern with media as human extensions leading to a collective consciousness brings us to a consideration of C. G. Jung's conception of the collective unconscious. McLuhan's views about modern society living mythically and in depth are complemented by Jungian thinking, and Langer's studies of human feeling are likewise complemented by the Jungian categories.

In human beings' continual expression of themselves in creativity, in their constant alteration of themselves through their extensions in media, do any discernible relationships persist throughout the transformation processes? If so, are these relationships evident in the structural elements of the art symbol? Here we must remind ourselves that any answer to such a question is purely theoretical; in other words, we must invent or find the categories in which such a problem might be explicated. We are at a level of abstraction and theorizing, which, far from ontologizing, has as its only goal speculative insight. The restrictions which we impose on our project at such a level are that our categories be relevant, consistent, illuminating, and demonstrable, that is, we should somehow bring them to bear not only on the problem at hand but in the last analysis on the work of art itself. The Jungian categories meet these specifications.

In asking whether any discernible relationships persist throughout human symbolic activity, we presume that the originative factor, the human individual, is expressed in this activity. While human creative potentiality seems infinite, nevertheless this potentiality has a range stemming primarily from the human biological condition. In Jungian thinking, human beings are coextensive with cosmos in the sense that the physical body shares all orders of being. The collective unconscious of humanity reaches to the furthest limits of the inanimate world as well as to the highest life forces. The projection of these two open ends of the human condition Jung describes in terms of the archetype of the shadow and the experience of transcendence. The tension of these two poles is the most radical one in the human psychic center. Another fundamental tension is the psychic center is the sexual one. Jung sees humanity in an original biological hermaphroditic condition. No matter what the level of physical or psychic development, a human being must continually come to terms with one's other half, with the woman within the man, or with the man within the woman. This tension Jung describes in the archetypes of anima and animus; the resolution of the tension he calls sygyzy. Another fundamental tension stems from the developmental process itself. As one comes to consciousness and to higher levels of consciousness, one must continually resolve the new level of experience with the contents of the unconscious. The resolution of this tension is expressed in symbols of unity found in all cultures. All of these tensions interact with each other and in Jungian thinking are said to be projected in human symbolic activity.[8] From our point of view they can be said to coincide with Langer's notion of "virtual tensions spanning tensions" in the structure of the art symbol. Thus far, we can say that if structural relations exist among art media, and if, as Langer holds, the structures of the arts are the organization of tensions as projections of feeling, and if, as McLuhan holds, all media are extensions of human beings, then these structural relations may be partially discerned through the categories describing the tensions at the human psychic center.

Jung holds that the archetypes have no content of themselves; they are rudimentary pathways of experience, of our feeling life. Hence, in studying the archetypes we must resort to human symbols. We cannot see directly into the human soul and pick out the tensions; instead, we must isolate the projections of tensions in symbols. The study of art symbols from this point of view, namely as projections of psychic tensions and their structural organization in different media, will provide a theoretical basis for approaching our problem.

Exactly how the anima-animus, shadow-transcendence tensions are projected in different media is difficult to say, for every work of art is unique. However, some general remarks can be made. The animus pole is felt as directed, forceful, didactic, functional, rational, serious, in addition to the usual feelings and emotions associated with masculine roles. The anima pole is felt as fanciful, imaginative, colorful, lyrical, light, intuitive, decorative, amusing, in addition to feelings and emotions associated with feminine roles. A work which is satisfying aesthetically has a resolution of the two, a sygyzy. The propensity for either pole is characteristic of different art styles. However, the anima-animus tension is only one among many; of primary importance is that the tensions and resolutions be felt.

Feelings of transcendence are feelings of positive energy, clarity, exaltation, faith, hope, renewal, love. Feelings at the shadow pole are feelings of darkness, desolation, despair, cruelty, hate, fear, destruction. The emotional tension of these polarities can be interwoven wth the anima-animus tension. Some anima feelings border on the shadow which would be irrationality and chaos leading to destruction and despair, while other anima feelings border on transcendence which would be feelings of inspiration and intuitive vision. Some animus feelings border on the shadow, such as, cruel cunning and brute force, and other animus feelings border on transcendence, such as, practical wisdom and positive creative activity. The shadow is not always simply negative, for it sometimes is manifested as childish and immature feelings. Transcendence is sometimes experienced not as opening vision, but as a violent breaking through rigid structures, as light creeping into darkness or just the faintest ray of hope.

Physical situations such as arrangements of space and the use of light and color can play upon these feelings in many ways, just as the arrangement of tones, melodies, and rhythms touch the diverse levels of emotional life. The only meaningful way to talk about these antinomies is to use them in clarifying one's authentic feeling response to a given work of art. If one cannot feel the work of art, the terms are empty, for this method of analysis demands psychic involvement. In effect, the work of art evokes one's feelings which are interpreted in the art symbol through the Jungian categories.

The best way to clarify this approach is throgh the use of examples. The illustrations used in this chapter are medieval architecture and music and the late Baroque singing voice. Other periods of art history are equally relevant.

In early Christian art the projection of feeling seems primarily the shadow-transcendence tension; it is expressive of the cultural preoccupation with salvation. The anima-animus tension is minimized. Hence, the art of this period is simplified and heavy in feeling, but the heaviness is counter-balanced by the feeling of transcendence. This description fits the early Christian church as well as the music, the chant or plainsong, of the period.

The early Roman Christian church was patterned after the Roman basilica and constructed in the post and lintel method using stone or brick.[9] Inside, the higher central nave section carries the movement of space upward toward the illumination provided by the clerestory windows. The feeling of the interior is thus upward toward the dominant source of light, symbolic of transcendence. On the horizontal plane, the structure has a symmetrical T-plan with the movement in space toward the half-round apse at the east containing the altar. The movement within most of the early churches is from east to west as though following the course of the sun, the ancient symbol of transcendence. East was also the direction of Palestine, the Holy Land or Sacred Center. Frequently an image of Christ (in Jungian terms a symbol of the transcendent self) adorned the east wall over the apse. The mosaics inside the early churches are archaic in style and convey religious themes; the colors of the mosaics are often stark and brilliant. The entire structure of the early church as patterned after the Roman law court building (which served an animus or masculine function) can be viewed as a projection of the animus archetype. Little projection of the anima is evident.

The early Church music shares the feeling level of the architecture and carries the dominant projection of the shadow-transcendence tension and the animus archetype. The plain-song, or sung prayer, was an unaccompained unisonous, monodic, unmeasured melody whose function was to make more potent the meanings of the liturgical text. These primitive melodies are characterized by their simplicity, depth, and robustness. Their structure usually fell into two styles; the syllabic style in which for the most part each syllable of the text is set to one note, with an occasional syllable set to two or three notes, and the melismatic style in which the syllables are set to two or more notes and groups of notes. The movement in both styles is upward and downward within a range. The Latin language contributed to the rhythmic flow of these melodies. In the responsorial chant a group of voices respond to a soloist, while the antiphonal chant features alternate singing of two groups of voices. In the monasteries where the chant was later perfected all the voices are masculine and uniform.[10] Despite the narrow artistic range of this music and its plaintive quality, the feeling level has great depth. The shadow-transcendence antinomy is evoked as one listens to this music, and one cannot help being moved. The male voices in unison reach up and down without relief. No sygyzy with the anima occurs in this art form. Indeed, the very absence of sygyzy provokes the sexual tension and forces a sublimation of the anima.

In a later period (before and including the twelfth century) in the Romanesque churches[11] the projection of anima is felt in the round arches and vaulted ceilings giving a higher and lighter feeling to the interior. However, the heavy buttressing of the exterior walls and the heavy interior walls and columns still emphasize the animus archetype. The horizontal space is altered with the elongated transcept and enlarged chevet. This cross shape of the interior space with the altar toward the center can be viewed as a mandala symbol, or symbol of unity, which, according to Jung, expresses a resolution of the sense of the center of consciousness with the expanding horizons of conscious experience. According to Jung, symbols of unity occur during the great psychic need to synthesize the inner and outer worlds of experience. Perhaps the collective psychic need for integration during this period followed upon the civilization of barbarian tribes and was expressed in the emergence of the monastic and manorial communities which utilized the Romanesque church.

The beginnings of polyphony in the church music of this period also reflect the projection of the anima archetype. A new art began to emerge in the practice of singing a florid melody in the upper part against the sustained tones of a Gregorian melody in the lower part. Emphasis was placed on ternary rhythm, the division of durational values into threes, whose rationalization was found in the dogma of the Holy Trinity. Here we have the beginnings of "tensions spanning tensions" as the anima archetype and the growing complexity of the inner psychic tension is projected in the art.

In the Gothic cathedrals we find a high degree of complexity in the projection of tensions.[12] The high vaulted ceilings and pointed arches are transcendent in feeling, and the light, color, and airiness of the great walls of stained glass give evidence of the developing projection of the anima. Indeed, anima is vividly affirmed in the naming of many of these cathedrals as "Notre Dame." The heaviness of the animus is gone; the fortified exterior walls have given way to flying buttresses. The higher level of animus is felt in the refined design and carefully executed structural elements of this architecture. The plan is more complex, yet highly functional. The highly developed skills of many artisans—sculptors, glazers, metal workers—are in evidence in every detail of these churches, as sygyzies within sygyzy. The feeling of this architecture is of wholeness and transcending joy.

Betty Burke

St. Peter's Basilica, Rome
Peterborough Cathedral, England
Typical Gothic, France

The church music of the late Gothic period reflects the same high level of artistic complexity. In the fourteenth century the new art emerges in the polyphonic Mass. The great four-part Mass, composed by Guillaume de Machaut (c. 1300-77) for the coronation of Charles V in 1364 is characteristic of this music. It is written in the prevailing motet style in which a tenor is featured, and the entire Mass achieves a sense of unity through the employment of diverse melodic formulas in the different sections.[13] The tensions, sygyzies, and transcendence of this music fit the feeling level of the great Gothic cathedrals.

In the Baroque period, the unique level of psychic integration of the late Gothic era is finished. The art is often florid, affected, and superficial. Of particular interest to our study is the beginning of a new development in the evolution of singing. In late Baroque music, we find the emergence of the voice of the third sex, the castrato, bringing a new dimension in human communication.[14] It is the voice of the hermaphrodite which expresses a symbolic language of the human race. The Baroque preoccupation with mythological material— the subject matter of the opera—reflects the emergence of the deeper stratum of the collective unconscious. The voice of the castrato has an abstract connotation, beyond the dichotomy of male and female, which communicates the forgotten language of myths and feelings in the deeper stratum of the unconscious. This was a new medium of commuication. In Jungian psychology, the hermaphrodite is symbolic of the original sygyzy of the deeper self found in all ancient cultures. This symbol of psychic unity emerges from the collective unconscious in times of distress as the great healer, as the unifying principle. The castrato voice of Baroque vocal music performed such a function. The musical revolution of the Baroque made the upper part the leading one, reducing the importance of all others. It alone gave personal expression and emotional range, while the tenor and basso were regarded as coarse and rough. Primitive peoples also prefer the high voice and regard the deep ones as grotesque. The castrato voice expressed a godlike character; its unique nature cast a spell over its hearers. Gluck's *Orfeo* was written for the castrato voice; its moving arias evoke feelings of sublimated grief and super-human effort. When a tenor or a contralto sings this part today, a level of abstraction provided by the castrato voice is lacking.

I have used the above examples to clarify my approach to the problem or structural relations among art media. Following Langer's thesis that the structures of the arts consist in the organization of tensions as projections of feeling, and McLuhan's theory of media as human extensions, we find in the Jungian categories meaningful ways of explicating these "organizations of tensions" and "projections of feelings." In feeling the psychic climate of a particular age through its art symbols and in clarifying these feelings through relevant categories, one can identify sets of structural elements in different media which project similar feelings. Thus, correspondences of formal elements can be said to hold among different media; these relationships cannot be seen as logical equivalences, and empirically they can be dismissed as depending at best upon an *ad hoc* hypothesis. Nevertheless, the correspondences can be established by a type of analogical reasoning in which the prime analogue is a core of human feeling. This method is like the habit of mind employed in aesthetic experience. However, in the fusion of medium and feeling, feelings are transformed and expanded, new horizons are opened, new possibilities of experience are explored, and hence final reductions are meaningless. In conclusion, the suggested resolution of the problem put forth in this chapter begins with the actual experience of feelings as in aesthetic experience and moves to a study of human beings in their most profound feeling states through relevant means and categories, thus providing an approach in aesthetic theory in which the study of structures in art media can be more fully developed.

CHAPTER 7

All references to C. G. Jung's works, unless otherwise indicated, are taken from the *Collected Works* (C. W.) second edition, 20 vols., Princeton University Press.

1. Susanne K. Langer, *Mind: An Essay on Human Feeling* (Baltimore: John Hopkins Press, 1967), Vol. 1, p. 158.

2. *Ibid.* p. 181.

3. *Ibid.* p. 186.

4. Marshall McLuhan, *Understanding Media: The Extensions of Man* (New York: McGraw-Hill Book Co., 1964), p. 13.

5. *Ibid.* p. 80.

6. *Ibid.* p. 25.

7. *Ibid.* p. 5.

8. C. W.; also, Carl G. Jung and M.-L. von Franz, Joseph L. Henderson, Jolande Jacobi, Aniela Jaffe, *Man and his Symbols* (Garden City, N. Y.: Doubleday & Co., Inc., 1964).

9. Examples of such churches are Sant Apollinare in Classe (533-536) Ravenna, Italy, St. Paul's Outside the Walls (386) Rome, destroyed by fire in 1823 and restored; and Old St. Peter's erected in Rome by Constantine and later torn down to make way for the present cathedral.

10. Examples of this type of music can be found in Gregorian chant which is preserved and still sung in Benedictine monasteries (e.g., Solesmes, France) and Trappist monasteries (e.g., Gethsemane, Kentucky). See Dom Anselm Hugh, "Early Medieval Music up to 1300" *New Oxford History of Music,* Vol. 11 (London: Oxford University Press, 1954). Also Percy C. Buck, *Oxford History of Music* (London: Oxford University Press, 1929).

11. Typical examples are St.-Etienne Abbay-aux-Hommes begun 1068, Caen, France; Ste. Trinité Abbaye-aux-Dames begun 1062, Caen, France; Mont St. Micheal Abbey Church, France, ca. 1100; St. Alban's Abbey, England, 1077; Mainz Cathedral, Germany, eleventh and twelfth centuries. See Kenneth John Conant, *Carolingian and Romanesque Architecture, 800 to 1200* (Baltimore: Penquin Books, 1959).

12. Examples are the great cathedrals of France, such as, Chartres, Amiens, Notre Dame de Paris, Reims, Rouen; Westminster Abbey, London; and the Cathedral of Cologne, Germany. See Robert Banner, *Gothic Architecture* (New York: George Braziller, 1961); Charles Herbert Moore, *Development and Character of Gothic Architecture* (London: Macmillan and Co., 1890).

13. See Manfred Bukofzer, *Studies in Medieval and Reenaissance Music* (New York: W. W. Norton and Co., 1950). Also H. E. Wooldridge, *The Oxford History of Music* (London: Oxford University Press, 1929), Vol. 1: *The Polyphonic Period.*

14. Paul J. Moses, "The Psychology of the Castrato Voice," *International Journal of Phoniatry, XII, 3, pp. 204-216.*

CHAPTER 8

FOUNDATIONS OF EDUCATION:

C.G. Jung's Typology and Its Education Implications*

Benjamin S. Bloom's *Taxonomy of Educational Objectives* has served as a touchstone in the orientation of educational goals and activities for the last two decades. While these objectives are organized into three broad domains—cognitive, affective, and psychomotor—little differentiation appears among them relative to different ways of perceiving the world, ways which include fundamentally different orientations to time, space, and life events. In all three domains, emphasis and development of activities relative to cognitive objectives clearly dominate educational goals. The affective domain, which includes interests, attitudes, values, appreciations, and adjustments, is conceived of as tightly intertwined with the cognitive domain, with each serving sometimes as a means to the other.[1]

A classification of objectives relative to the third domain, the manipulative and motor-skills area, has more recently been developed.[2] Here also the cognitive domain appears of primary importance, the general premise being that movement efficiency promotes cognitive development. Most perceptual motor programs are based upon the notion that structural movement experiences improve perceptual abilities and perhaps facilitate cognitive development. Thus all three domains are perceived from a cognitive perspective in

*First published by the South Atlantic Philosophy of Education Society. *Proceedings* of the Twenty-Third Annual Meeting on Teaching and Philosophy, Oct. 5-7, 1978 (Richmond, Va.: Virginia Commonwealth Univ., 1979).

which time, space, and events are experienced in a consistent manner. The basic orientation involves a linear view of time, a measurable view of space, and a sequential experience of life events, which can be ordered, classified, and valued objectively.

In Jung's topology this manner of perception would fall into the category of what he calls the thinking function. However, Jung has three other basic psychological functions: sensation, feeling, and intuition. Each of the four functions involves a different space-time orientation with even further differentiation made possible through the added factors of introversion and extraversion. The complexity of these different psychological bases of experience has implications for far-reaching effects on educational goals and methods. An awareness of some of these implications has prompted me to pursue the theme of this chapter.

My method is first to outline Jung's psychological functions along with the characteristics of individuals dominated by a particular function (called psychological types) and second to suggest implications relative to methods and goals of education.

To present the complexity of Jung's topology in a few brief pages is difficult. Let us begin with an image of wholeness comprised of a center and a periphery with four different directions, each having an outer and an inner aspect. I am describing a symbol of totality—in Jungian terms, a mandala symbol. Jung conceives of the human individual in this way, as a center of wholeness with four basic functions, each capable of receiving and responding to inner and outer stimuli. A human individual achieves ego identity, growth, and maturity in life through the exercise of the inner and outer aspects of these four basic psychological functions. The inner and outer aspects of the functions are called introversion and extraversion. The functions themselves can be thought of as opposite pairs of opposite functions. The opposite pairs are called the rational and irrational functions; the rational functions are thinking and feeling which are diametrically opposed to each other, while the irrational functions are sensation and intuition which are also opposite to each other. Each of the four functions can be either introverted or extra-verted; each carries with it a different mode of being in the world, that is, a different way of experiencing time and space and relating to situations and events. The variety of these modes of being in the world is unknown to the individual who consciously experiences life principally from the perspective of the primary function. Until one's capacities for experience are widened, one remains ignorant of the possible ways that other people function. Let us now review brief descriptions of the four basic functions and their corresponding types.[3]

Extraverted thinking is oriented by objective data, while intro-verted thinking is oriented by subjective factors. The extraverted type strives to bring one's total life-activities into relation with intellectual conclusions which are based on facts or generally valid ideas. For the introverted thinking type, facts are of secondary importance; new views, new questions, new theories, new insights are this person's main concerns. Both extraverted and introverted thinking types relate to time in a linear fashion; things are experienced in terms of relating past to present to future in what has been termed the time line.

Thinking types are interested primarily in the flow of process rather than in discrete events. The ongoing situation in its totality is of more importance than any single moment, episode, or happening. This lack of enthusiasm for the particular event at the moment gives rise to the criticism that the thinking types are cold, detached, uncaring. However, their interest lies in the whole process, and thus their delight and excitement must be projected through time. Their joy is proportional to the scope of process that can be glimpsed in any set of events.

Because thinking types care so much about continuity and

consistency, they tend to live according to principles. Spontaneity is often lacking in their actions; they must make up their minds and arrive at logical conclusions before they act. Thus, they are often ineffective in crisis situations and tend to be over-scrupulous.

On the positive side, these types do not blunder into situations thoughtlessly; they avoid waste, danger and error. They are good at planning; they are punctual and respect time. The attention to process, the love of planning, the respect for principles—these characteristics of thinking types stem from their temporal orientation.

The exact opposite of the thinking type is the feeling type. Jung calls both of these types rational functions because they are concerned with ordering reality: the thinking type does so according to ideas, theories, and principles; the feeling type accomplishes order by evaluating events, people, and situations according to emotional responses. Since to order simultaneously in two conflicting ways is not possible, a person having a primary thinking function would tend to be weak in the area of feeling, and vice versa.

Extraverted feeling is oriented by objective values, while introverted feeling is oriented by subjective factors. Both feeling types are well aware of emotional currents; the maintenance of relationships is of central importance to them. They tend to see the events of the world in personal terms. Their motivations are usually to heighten emotion, to achieve a satisfactory memory, or to intensify the interpersonal atmosphere. They do not act in a detached way because of principles (as do thinking types) or because of practicality (as do sensation types) or simply out of a desire to make things more exciting (as do intuitive types).

For the feeling type, time is circular; the past manifests itself in the present, and the experience is immediately returned to the past as a memory. Feeling types see situations in terms of what is similar to events of their personal past rather than in terms of what is unique about the existential situation. The new is not experienced as being novel; instead, it is related to the known, the previously experienced, and familiar. Feeling types tend to be uncomfortable in new situations and to delay making decisions which would change their lives greatly. Newness or rapid change signifies that one is ignoring, overthrowing, or disregarding commitments which had once been chosen as the appropriate and moral way to behave. Thus, feeling types become trapped in remembrance of things past.

On the positive side, because feeling types are so well aware of emotional currents, they can influence the behavior of others, and the more extraverted they are, the more successful they are in doing so. Both introverted and extraverted types are capable of subtly influencing a situation, bringing to it warmth, joy, freshness, conviviality, companionship, and cohesion.

Feeling types are able to respond to the needs of others and to disregard other requirements in order to meet them. To develop a language of the heart, rather than of the mind, is the goal of those with a primary feeling function. Poetry is the natural expression of this function, as history is of the thinking function, technology of the sensation function, and fantasy of intuition.

Jung call sensation and intuition irrational functions since both of these functions enable a person to be open and receptive to outer and inner stimuli without the immediate ordering factors of thinking and feeling. As irrational functions, sensation and intuition are repressed whenever the rational functions, thinking or feeling, dominated the personality. The irrational functions can become conscious only insofar as the rational attitude of consciousness permits accidental perceptions and intuitions to become conscious contents and insofar as these contents are realized through symbolic manifestations.

Sensation is a vital function equipped with the strongest vital instinct. No other human type can equal the extraverted sensation-type in realism. In the introverted attitude, sensation undergoes a considerable modification because the subjective factor alters the sense perception at its very source. A true sense perception exists, but objects are not seen as forcing their way into the subject in their own right. Instead, the subject sees objects quite differently than the rest of humanity.

The subject perceives the same things as everybody else, but is more concerned with the significance and meaning of the subjective perception released by the objective stimulus. Thus sense impression for the introverted sensation type moves toward the depth of the meaningful, while the extraverted type seizes only the momentary and manifest existence of things.

Both introverted and extraverted sensation types experience time as the present. Linkage with the past is weak; hence they do not integrate past experiences into their present activities as much as do other types. Events are met in terms of their existential reality. Life is a happening: where it comes from and where it is going are not important. This lack of concern with the past or future and an almost total reliance on the present is the primary characteristic of the sensation type. For this type, all energy is concentrated in the present. Thus, this type is superbly effective in dealing with concrete reality. Nothing hampers individuals of this type from facing and dealing with the object or situation before them.

Sensation types are practical; ideas, feelings, and inspirations are not of primary importance to them. They can respond to the slightest cue, grasp the nature of a situation at a glance, and act without hesitation because the event itself tells them the correct behavior. They do not deliberate between alternative courses of action. They do not concern themselves with the way others feel, nor with thought about things. Instead, they act because action is the only appropriate response to the strength of stimuli.

The introverted type relates to the world in a slower manner than the extravert and tends to do things on a smaller scale, while the extraverted type is more concerned with power and with influencing a wider environment. A disadvantage of both types is the lack of a good sense of the future which is needed in situations such as long-range planning. However, the ability to read the depth of the present is their substitute for the lack of futurity.

The fourth function, intuition, is also considered by Jung an irrational function. This function transmits images to the conscious mind, images which concern relations or conditions of events which are not immediately discernible through any of the other functions. When intuition is given sufficient attention, these images have a decisive bearing upon action. In the extraverted attitude, intuition has an objective orientation and comes very close to sensation. However, sensation is used more as a direction point for distinct vision. The sensations of the intuitive type seem selected to encompass the greatest possibilities because only through awareness of possibilities is intuition fully satisfied.

The intuitive type is constantly seeking new outlets and fresh possibilities in external life. For this person stable conditions have an air of impending suffocation. This type seizes hold of new objects and new ways with intensity and enthusiasm, but will hold on to them only so long as they promise future development. However reasonable and opportune a situation may be, an intuitive type will abandon it without regard or remembrance as soon as the limits of the situation are clearly defined, for at that point the situation has become a prison. Consequently, this type is forever seeking possibilities; neither reason nor feeling are restraints, since these are inferior functions. Morality consists in a loyalty to an intuitive view of things and a voluntary submission to its authority.

Just as the extraverted intuitive shows a remarkable indifference to outer objects, the introverted intuitive shows the same indifference to inner objects. This type moves from image to image without establishing any personal connection with these inner experiences.

For this person the images are produced in inexhaustible abundance by the creative energy of life and have no immediate utility. The introverted intuitive function is the strangest of all to the outer world. However, without this function no prophets would exist. The inner experiences of this type are inherently related to general events. Often this type can foresee new possibilities in more or less clear outline, as well as events which later transpire.

Both intuitive types experience time as the future revealed in the present moment through the images which they experience. They cannot be motivated by concepts, ideals, feelings, memories, values, or pragmatic considerations. Their first loyalty is to their compelling experiences of images of the future and its possibilities.

I have briefly outlined the introverted and extraverted attitudes of the four functions and the corresponding types which result when one of the functions dominates the personality of an individual. However, in reality few pure types exist. Jung does hold, however, that every individual has a predominate type almost from birth, that is, an innate tendency to be introverted or extraverted and to have a preference for experiences attributable to one of the four functions. Babies do show remarkable differences and preferences from birth regardless of their environments, though not irrespectively of the influences of environment. Parents are often at a loss to understand how their children function, especially when a child is of a type opposite to their own. Jung holds that every individual has an innate capacity to experience the world in a certain way. If his hypothesis has any weight, then it would be of great value to understand a child's typology and to work with it from the very beginning of development. Jung believes that individuals have a primary function which is the basic ground of their relation to the world. In the course of their early lives, through education and life experiences, they develop what he calls auxiliary functions; these would be the functions closest to the primary one.

The system works this way: thinking and feeling are opposite types, as are sensation and intuition. For the thinking type, sensation and intuition would be auxiliary functions and feeling would be the opposite or inferior function, while for the feeling type, sensation and intuition also would be auxiliary functions and thinking would be the opposite of fourth function. For the sensation type, feeling and thinking would be auxiliary functions, and intuition would be the opposite or inferior function, while for intuition, thinking and feeling would be auxiliary functions and sensation would be the opposite or inferior function. If the primary function is extraverted, the inferior function is introverted; if the primary function is introverted, the inferior function is extraverted. Furthermore, the inferior function is conceived of as the hardest to develop and is not likely to be cultivated until the second half of life. However, when the auxiliary functions and finally the inferior function are all developed, then the individual experiences the most creative period of life and has become, as Jung would say, an individuated person. This individual has achieved a firm grounding of the ego in relation to the world, enabling one to function in highly differentiated ways and also has established contact with the deeper ground of one's being, bringing great inner peace and inspiration. The implications of this system of thought and this view of human beings for education are many and startling. I shall point out a few of them.

Unlike Bloom, Jung does not take thinking to be the primary function *per se* of human experience. Therefore, the first implication is that thinking need not or should not dominate all the other functions in the educational process. Indeed, the ideal would be that each individual develop one's primary function first and achieve a basic grounding of the ego, that is, a fundamental relatedness to the world, in that function. This would help bring about an initial psychic security so necessary for growth and development. Many children get off to a bad start in the educational process because of wrong experiences in kindergarten or first grade: the introverted intuitive child who is not ready for the extraverted sensation experiences of kindergarten, the highly gifted feeling-type child who through a bad relation to a first grade teacher has difficulty learning to read and thereafter learning problems, the extraverted sensation child, often called hyperkinetic, who can not slow down long enough to master cognitive skills. For the thinking type child, particularly, the extraverted type, learning comes easily in today's schools, for the whole system with its elaborate sets of tests and measurements is geared to this type. The rest of the types often eventually become labeled slow learners, problem children, etc. Because these children are forced by a system of education to undergo a kind of development unsuited to their individual typologies and consequently their ego needs at the time, and because they are very early imprisoned in a value structure which favors the thinking type and its activities (cognitive skills, goals, and ideals), these children often become behavioral problems, dropouts, and misfits.

In describing the different types, Jung felt himself at a loss because he believed that only a feeling type could adequately delineate a feeling type and so on.

The development of the feeling function is concerned not only with the cultivation of one's capability to have feeling experiences, but also with the structuring, refinement, and evaluation of these experiences. Feeling is concerned with human relatedness to objects, situations, and other persons. Certain forms of feeling can be taught: awareness of others, manners, courtesy, tact, etc. Children can be put through the motions of these empty forms of experience. The actual feeling experiences that ideally go along with gestures such as a handshake, a thank you, an apology, a movement of respect may not come until much later in a child's development. However, by teaching a child these forms of human relatedness through performance rather than through cognition one provides the channels for possible experiences later. With no experience of feeling forms, just as with a lack of exposure to aesthetic forms, levels of experience are denied a child.

For a child whose primary function is feeling, cognitive skills should not be pushed beyond the child's capability to integrate the feeling tone of the learning situation. Timed tests, competitive cognitive activities, hostile environments—all situations in which the feeling climate is neglected or repressed—result in poor learning or no learning at all for the feeling type. A feeling type child in first grade can learn to read if not pushed, if the child loves the teacher, and if the emotional climate of the home is good. The child may not learn as quickly as the thinking type, but chances are that this child will advance in social skills much more rapidly than classmates of all other types.

On the other hand, activities associated with the development of the feeling function *per se* need to be designed for all educational levels. The development, refinement, and evaluation of human feeling is the most sadly neglected area of education today—a modern wasteland left to psychotherapy, medicine, social agencies, and criminal justice. Statistics indicate a marked increase in the phenomonon of sociopathology. This situation, formerly known as psychopathic deviation and earlier as moral insanity, has to do with an inadequate feeling function. Physiological reasons may exist for this pathology, but psychological reasons also exist, which include the fact that in many cases some capabilities for human experience have never been developed.

In classical educational systems, the development of the feeling function was brought about through the cultivation of the moral virues. In Aristotle's *Nicomachean Ethics*[4] this aspect of education is outlined; sensitivity to the feeling level or to the appropriate form of behavior in any given social situation varied according to the dynamics of the moment. The key concept was the "golden mean" which meant a sense of how to act and what to do in any given context. Initially, virtues were cultivated through imitation of appropriate forms of behavior. However, moral maturity was achieved when the individual had developed the feelings to go with the cultivated forms. Virtue was conceived of as an art or skill of behavior to be developed in the context of one's entire social situation, including its many and varied obligations. Finding the "golden mean" in any given instance would be different for every individual because every individual life is different. Aristotle's *Ethics* is a prime example of the education of the feeling function, though not necessarily an appropriate example for our times. Let us look at other implications of Jung's theory.

The sensation function in relation to educational goals and methods is concerned with the cultivation of diverse skills of perception and with activities related to concrete objects or situations. When sensation function activities are designed solely to enhance the cognitive domain, then opportunities for the full development of this function are neglected. At the present time, many perceptual activities are geared to cognitive outcomes, such as training in seeing formal structural relationships among objects, and so on. However beneficial this type of training in perception may be for cognitive learning, it can be detrimental to the formation of artistic or aesthetic perception which requires an awareness of the unique. In aesthetic experience, the individual must be disengaged from all cognitive associations and goals. One must learn to see objects in and for themselves. One must use what aestheticians call the "logic of the imagination" which involves the development of the appreciator's own unique subjective responses and the delineation of these responses as analogues of the aesthetic object.[5]

The cultivation of the sensation function is accomplished to a great degree through activities leading to proficiency in the arts, crafts, trades, and sports where the body and body skills are of prime importance. In all of these areas, cognitive skills are necessary, but the "doing" as much as the "knowing" is important.

Hyperkinetic children can be described as having a pronounced extraverted sensation function. When these children are locked into an educational value structure geared to the thinking type, they usually suffer frustration and loss of self-esteem. They are often forced to suppress their strong physical energies in favor of mental activities for which they may have very little aptitude. They may be labeled slow learners, and they often become disciplinary problems. These children could learn to use their body skills in highly developed ways which would bring much happiness to themselves and to society. They can also learn cognitive and social skills if these are not forced on them as of primary importance. The highly developed skills necessary in arts, crafts, sports, trades, and technologies which are needed in today's society demand the type of physical talent which sensation types often have by nature.

Finally, the intuitive type. Little place or time is given for the cultivation of the intuitive type in today's educational system. One may be labeled the dreamer or the fool. More often one is the dropout. One fits in nowhere. One's mind is filled with questions and wonder, with dreams and fantasies, with a general sense of unreality. One does not seem to belong. At least one child of this type is in every class. What does one do with this child and with all other children who from time to time manifest these tendencies?

The system to which the intuitive must conform is highly structured with programs, goals, schemes, planned activities, tests, and final grades. Most of it is meaningless to this child who lives in a wider reality where all of this seems petty and unimportant. Parents and teachers worry, but no one knows what to do. What *can* one do?

First, one can try to understand where the child is and allow the child to be there. One can recognize that this child lives in a different world with a different sense of time and reality and consequently with a different set of values. One can accept and let be what the child is. This child must be given space to dream. When the pressure to learn and to conform is off, the natural curiosity of this child will be the motivation to master cognitive skills in order to satisfy curiosity. The child may then become the top student of the class. The thinking function may then be developed in order pursue fantasies and intuitions. One cannot force the child to learn through threats, promises, or rewards, but one can tempt the child to learn. One can stimulate curiosity, a sense of wonder, and fantasy. Then the child will boldly take up the challenge. This is the child who will benefit from individually planned studies to express inner experiences. Often such children are brilliant, but not necessarily adept in cognitive activities. They need only to be recognized, stimulated, encouraged, and given opportunities to pursue their development in their own unique ways.

Today's educational system has neither understanding nor recognition of the intuitive function, and no educational activities are designed for its development. I fear that this complete suppression of a natural human function is compensated by the outbreak of drug abuse. For many young people, drugs are the only available means of exploring the sensational, the fantastic, the cosmic, and other higher dimensions of human consciousness—all expressions of the intuitive function.

Thus far, I have isolated the four basic psychological types, but a little of each type is in every student. Educators should be trained to recognize these types of behavior in their students and especially to recognize the primary psychological function of each individual early in the educational process in order to give individuals a chance to grow in and strengthen their basic typologies. Thus the necessary ego formation could be helped. With later development of auxiliary functions through the cultivation of wider educational goals and methods, the individual would experience a sense of fulfillment and completion. Jung holds that the full development of the fourth function, the opposite function of one's type, often called the inferior function, is usually reserved for the second half of life. Perhaps this is the psychological justification for continuing education.

If the cognitive domain (the thinking function in Jung's scheme) were dethroned in the educational system, so that other activities and goals of education could assume their rightful importance, then a truly democratic education would be possible. Equal opportunity for all to pursue cognitive goals and ideals is not enough. All human activities have their value and worth in the development of an individual life and in the harmonious functioning of society. Educators, who themselves most frequently belong to the thinking type, are often guilty of imposing their typology and the values that go with it on all indiscriminately. Consequently, the values of the society have become unbalanced. Few are adequately trained to pursue, value, and enjoy the skills so needed in a smoothly functioning society. Basic forms of feeling necessary for relating to others and for happy daily living have been neglected. Creative insight and fantasy have been repressed by pragmatic demands with resulting boredom, frustration, and often violence. What is needed is a broader view of human nature and more imaginative concepts of education. C.G. Jung's topology is a step in this direction.

CHAPTER 8

All references to C. G. Jung's works, unless otherwise indicated, are taken from the *Collected Works* (C. W.) second edition, 20 vols., Princeton University Press.

1. Benjamin S. Bloom, ed., *Taxonomy of Educational Objectives: The Classification of Educational Goals* Handbook I: Cognitive Domain by a Committee of College and University Examiners (New York: David McKay Co., 1956). David R. Krathwohl; Benjamin S. Bloom and Bertram B. Masia, *Taxonomy of Educational Goals* Handbook II: Affective Domain (New York: David McKay Co., 1964).

2. Anita J. Harrow, *A Taxonomy of the Psychomotor Domain: A Guide for Developing Behavioral Objectives* (New York: David McKay Co., 1972). Elizabeth Jane Simpson, *The Classification of Educational Objectives: Psychomotor Domain* (University of Illinois Research Project No. OE 5-85-104, 1966).

3. Jung's Topology has been the subject of much commentary and additional development by Jungians. The primary source for this presentation is Jung's work: "General Description of the Types" (1960), C. W. 6:330-407 (556-671). See also James Hillman, "The Feeling Function," *Lectures on Jung's Topology* (New York: Spring Publications, 1971). James Hillman, "Types, Images, and the Vision of Completeness" (New York: C. G. Jung Foundation, Audio Tape # 012, 1977). Michael Malone, *Psycho-types* (New York: Dutton, 1977). Harriet Mann, Miriam Siegler, and Humphrey Asmond, "The Many Worlds of Time," *Journal of Analytical Psychology* (January 1968), 33-35. Marie-Louise von Franz, "The Inferior Function," *Lectures on Jung's Topology* (New York: Spring Publications, 1971).

4. Aristotle, "Nichomachean Ethics," *Basic Works* edited by Richard McKeon (New York: Random House, 1941) pp. 935-1112.

5. Edward G. Ballard, *Art and Analysis: An Essay Toward a Theory in Aesthetics* (The Hague: Martinus Nijhoff, 1957). Susanne K. Langer, *Problems of Art: Ten Philosophical Lectures* (New York: Charles Scribner's Sons, 1957).

CHAPTER 9

EDUCATION FOR THE MATURER YEARS:

C. G. Jung on Education for
the Second Half of Life

In this chapter, I will relate some of C. G. Jung's ideas to the question of education for the second half of life, a period which for Jung meant any time from the age of thirty-five onward. In developing this topic, I shall first give an overview of Jung's model of the human personality with implications for education in the maturer years, and secondly, I shall recount what Jung wrote on this subject.

C. G. Jung's conceptual model of the human personality is an idea of wholeness which is achieved through the development of all facets of one's being, as well as through the resolution of opposing experiential forces. This theme of opposites, which in Western philosophy goes back to pre-Socratic thinkers, and in Eastern religions is manifested in concepts such as tao and rta, is central to Jung's understanding of reality in general and the human situation in particular.

Jung saw the human individual as having four main psychological functions: thinking, feeling, sensation, and intuition. In relationship to each other, these psychological dimensions can be thought of as opposite pairs of opposite functions. Thinking and feeling, which are opposite to each other, are called rational functions because they order inner and outer stimuli. The thinking function orders conceptually, while the feeling function orders according to values based upon emotional responses. Opposed to this pair of opposites are the irrational functions, sensation and intuition, which in turn are opposite to each other. These functions are considered irrational because they are open to the indiscriminate flow of outer and inner impulses, the sensation function being associated with outer stimuli and intuition with inner inspirations and psychic states. Additional psychologically determining factors are extraversion and introversion, with a native predominance of one over the other as part of one's basic orientation to life.

These functions related to educational endeavors can be associated as follows: thinking with science, mathematics, logic, and all purely conceptual areas of study; feeling with poetry, music, art, literature, all areas of development concerned primarily with human emotions and values; sensation with technology, crafts, sports, and all endeavors involving body skills; and intuition with religion, speculative philosophy, creative inspiration, and the development of higher levels of consciousness. Jung believed that every individual is born with a predominant function which becomes the foundation of one's primary orientation to life, and that in the course of living and in the process of education, auxiliary functions are developed. He made the point that the fourth function, that is, the function which is the direct opposite of one's native one, is the hardest to develop, and that growth through this function usually does not come about until the second half of life. In addition, this fourth function is always manifested in a manner opposite to the basic one, so that, for example, if one's basic psychological orientation were introverted thinking, one's fourth function would be manifested as extraverted feeling, or if one's basic orientation were extraverted sensation, one's fourth function would show itself as introverted intuition, and so on.

The need to develop the fourth function usually asserts itself, often in an overwhelming way, at the beginning of the second half of life. When individuals at this period change their outlooks on life, their values, their professions, and perhaps their mates and lifestyles, an explanation from the Jungian point of view is that they are trying to satisfy needs which cannot be met with the orientation of their earlier years.

Of the "inferior" functions which often lag behind in the process of differentiation, Jung said,

> Experience shows that it is practically im
> possible, owing to adverse circumstances in
> general, for anyone to develop all his psycho
> logical functions simultaneously. The de
> mands of society compel a man to apply
> himself first and foremost to the differentia
> tion of the function with which he is best
> equipped by nature, or which will secure
> him the greatest social success. Very fre
> quently, indeed as a general rule, a man
> identifies more or less completely with the
> most favored and hence the most developed
> function....As a consequence of this one-
> sided development, one or more functions
> are necessarily retarded. These functions
> may properly be called *inferior* in a psycho
> logical but not psychopathological sense,
> since they are in no way morbid but merely
> backward as compared with the favored
> function.[1]

From the point of view of Jung's model of the human personality, upon arrival at the threshold of middle life, one would have two fundamental needs for further education: first, additional training for the development of "inferior" psychological functions which have been neglected in the youthful period of life, and later, education for what Jung called the mature years, the years in which an individual realizes a more complete potentiality in oneself through study, reflection, creativity, and culture, a period which culminates finally in a meaningful death.

Colleges and universities, especially those in urban areas, are for the most part aware of the first need. Enrollments show a marked increase in numbers of "older" students—those individuals who want further training in order to change professions or to update professional skills, as well as others who simply want to broaden their knowledge and understanding in general. Institutions of higher learning usually make no special concessions to these individuals in terms of specially designed courses or methods of learning suitable to people of maturer years; nevertheless, these students are not discriminated against because of age. However, if educators were to look more closely at the needs of maturer students, they would discover much room for improvement and creativity in regard to policies, course offerings, and methods of instruction.

Let us consider the second need of the mature student, the need of the individual who is beyond the necessity of bringing to consciousness the exercise of all the psychological functions for professional or personal reasons. Let us look at the individual who is in the individuation process (to use Jung's terminology). According to Jung, this person has a still further need of education in order to deepen one's understanding of the meaning of life and in order to participate more fully in the life of culture. Of these individuals, Jung said,

> There are large numbers of people for whom the development of individuality is the prime necessity, especially in a cultural epoch like ours, which is literally flattened out by collective norms....there are, among people of maturer age, very many for whom the development of individuality is an indispensable requirement. Hence I am privately of the opinion that it is just the mature person who, in our times, has the greatest need of

some further education in individual culture after his youthful education in school and university has moulded him on exclusively collective lines and thoroughly imbued him with the collective mentality. I have often found that people of riper years are in this respect capable of education to a most unexpected degree, although it is just those matured and strengthened by the experience of life who resist most vigorously the purely reductive standpoint.[2]

By "the purely reductive standpoint," I interpret Jung to mean the standpoint of science and academia generally which would reduce all phenomena to theories, principles, and laws. While this point of view is necessary and vital to an understanding of reality, it needs to be complemented by other perspectives. Precisely these "other" dimensions of understanding the maturer individual needs most.

Jung held that an individual in the second half of life, because of the diminishing powers of one's organism, needs to subordinate instincts to cultural goals. He felt that because individuals are unaware of the nature of their needs at this time and consequently continue to try to live with youthful aims rather than with goals suitable to their stage of development, much disappointment, frustration, boredom, and sense of meaninglessness ensue. Unfortunately, intelligent and cultivated people often live their lives without even knowing of the possibility of such transformation and embark upon the second half of life wholly unprepared. Consequently, many are wrecked during the transition from the biological to the cultural sphere. Furthermore, collective education makes no provision for this transitional period. Jung asked.

Or are there perhaps colleges for forty-year-olds which prepare them for the coming life and its demands as the ordinary colleges introduce our young people to a knowledge of the world? No, thoroughly unprepared we step into the afternoon of life; worse still, we take this step with the false assumption that our truths and ideals will serve us as hitherto. But we cannot live the afternoon of life according to the programme of life's morning; for what was great in the morning will be little at evening, and what in the morning was true will at evening have become a lie. I have given psychological treatment to too many people of advancing years, and have looked too often into the secret chambers of their souls, not to be moved by this fundamental truth.[3]

Jung believed that aging people should know that their lives are not mounting and expanding but that an inexorable inner process enforces the contraction of life. A human being would do well to realize longevity has meaning for the species and that the afternoon of life must also have its significance and cannot be merely a pitiful appendage of life's morning. Therefore, the aging person has a duty and a necesity to devote serious attention to oneself; whereas, Jung said that for a young person to be too preoccupied with oneself is a danger and almost a sin.

If young people are so preoccupied with themselves that they hold back from life and do not allow their creative potentialities to catch fire and be consumed, then they see in old age a mere diminuation of life and feel earlier ideals only as something faded and worn out. Whereas, if a person fills up the beaker of life and empties it to the lees, then the quiet of old age will be very welcome. Jung said that for many people all too much unlived life remains over, "...sometimes potentialities which they could never have lived with the best of wills, so that they approach the threshold of old age with unsatisfied demands which inevitably turn their glances backward...."[4]

Jung held, however, that for such people to look back is fatal; therefore, a prospect and a goal in the future are absolutely necessary for them. If they are not to look backwards, then, what can they look forward to? If one does not look backward to youth, can one only looks forward to death? Yes, Jung took death and its meaning to be the goal of the second half of life. He said.

> As a doctor I am convinced that it is hygenic— if I may use that word—to discover in death a goal towards which one can strive, and that shrinking away from it is something unhealthy and abnormal which robs the second half of life of its purpose. I therefore consider that all religions with a supramundane goal are eminently reasonable from the point of view of psychic hygiene. When I live in a house which I know will fall about my head within the next two weeks, all my vital functions will be impaired by this thought; but if on the contrary I feel myself to be safe, I can dwell there in a normal and comfortable way. From the standpoint of psychotherapy it would therefore be desirable to think of death as only a transition, as part of a life process whose extent and duration are beyond our knowledge.[5]

To say that Jung saw the goal of the second half of life to be death would be an over-simplification. Instead, he meant the goal to be the discovery of the meaning of death in the context of life, and here the life of culture makes its strongest contribution. Hence the necessity of cultural aims. In the notion of culture, Jung included the symbolic transformations and creative achievements of all the great civilizations of the world. In studying the symbols of diverse cultures, Jung discovered deeper layers of psychological insight which not only contribute to his understanding of the meaning of life, but also shed light on the meaning of death. Jung saw life and death as part of a larger process in which the individual participates. Of death, he said, "...only he remains vitally alive who is ready to *die with life,*" and continued, "...not wanting to live is identical with not wanting to die."[6]

The implication of this positive meaning of death, namely, death as the ultimate goal of the second half of life and death as the culmination of the meaning of life, is of profound significance for education. In this context, I interpret Jung's ideas as pointing to a whole new project in higher education. Concretely, this might mean new programs of study in philosophy, psychology, comparative religions, the arts, mythology, anthropology, and the physical sciences in a humanistic perspective, programs designed to meet the needs of maturer people searching for the meaning of their individual lives within the broad spectrum of human culture. It would mean the development of methods of learning with emphasis on individual needs. It would mean new approaches to literature and the arts with emphasis on hermeneutic rather than traditionally critical and "scholarly" aims. It would mean an emphasis on the value of cultural goals for the enhancement of individual life and for the continual discovery of individual meanings, rather than for collective pragmatic ends. It would mean learning situations designed to bring about changes of attitude in regard to critical phases of life, such as, periods of deprivation, illness, and death. Above all, it would mean contributing to the change of a youth-oriented society to a social milieu with respect for age and a joyful anticipation of maturity.

132

CHAPTER 9

All references to C. G. Jung's works, unless otherwise indicated, are taken from the *Collected Works* (C. W.) second edition, 20 vols., Princeton University Press.

1. "Psychological Types" (1960), C. W., 6:230 (763).

2. "On Psychic Energy" (1928), C. W., 8:60 (112).

3. "The Stages of Life" (1933), C. W., 8:398-399 (784).

4. *Ibid.* 401 (789).

5. *Ibid.* 402 (792).

6. *Ibid.* 407 (800).

CHAPTER 10

BEYOND THE RATIONAL:

Jung and Mysticism

Sir Laurens Van der Post in his introduction to the BBC film *The Story of C.G. Jung* confesses that for many years he dismissed Jung as a "wooly mystic," never having met him or read his works. Such is a common attitude among people today. Was Jung a mystic or not? The answer depends on one's definition and application of the term mysticism. If one takes a current definition—the experience of mystical union or direct communion with ultimate reality reported by mystics, a religion based on mystical communion, a theory of mystical knowledge, a theory postulating the possibility of direct and intuitive acquisition of ineffable knowledge or power—and applies this label to Jung as an exclusive description of the man and his work, one is entirely wrong. Jung was not simply a mystic. He claimed that he was an empiricist—one interested in facts and in the data supporting those facts. His researches into the human psyche had to have continuity with both historical ideas and the findings of modern science. Yet Jung the man had a definite mystical side; in his personal life he did experience direct union with ineffable knowledge through his dreams, fantasies, and intuitions. An interior life not only influenced him personally, but also was a source of the creative genius in all of his work. As Jung said, the creative spirit brings forth what is new in the real sense of the word. This newness in part springs from an indefinable source, which Jung experienced in his life. Jung's autobiography is filled with examples supporting this point of view.

First, as a boy Jung felt an ineffable presence in nature, not only the exquisite beauty of trees, mountains, water, fire and stone, but something else, a mystery, an eternity. He described the experience of sitting on a stone for hours fascinated by the puzzle: "Am I the one who is sitting on the stone, or am I the stone on which *he* is sitting?"[1] Later in life returning to this spot Jung felt the world of his childhood as something eternal from which he had been wrenched away, a world where he experienced his first intimations of immortality.

From earliest childhood, too, Jung cultivated an interior life, a side of himself that was nourished with secret places, objects, and rituals. From the beginning occurred an innate sense of communion with an "other" which was ineffable, a mystery, a source of fascination and awe.

During Jung's later student years around 1898, he became acquainted with spiritualisitc phenomena through relatives, notably a girl of about fifteen. He was drawn into this situation through two extraordinary events taking place within two weeks: the first was the sudden splitting of a solid round walnut dining table in an adjoining room where his mother was sitting knitting, and the second was the spontaneous splitting of a steel bread knife in four pieces while the knife was lying in a bread basket in the dining room sideboard. Jung could find no cause or explanation of these events until he learned a few weeks later that his relatives who had been engaged in spiritualistic practices had been thinking of having him meet the medium who was the center of these activities. Jung then joined the group and turned his attention to the content of the communications and the limiting conditions imposed on the experiments. He later set forth the results of these observations in his doctoral thesis. Jung said that this was the one great experience which wiped out all of his earlier philosophy and made it possible for him to achieve a psychological point of view, for he had discovered some objective facts about the human psyche.[2] Later, when preparing himself for the state examinations in psychiatry, he read in the preface to one of the textbooks that psychiatry was in an incomplete state of development and that therefore its textbooks were stamped with a more or less subjective character. Jung realized that in psychiatry alone could the two currents of his interests flow together: the empirical field common to both biological and spiritual facts. One cannot say simply that the above observations are indicative of a mystical character, but they do show that Jung's rational mind could accommodate irrational facts and that he was interested above all in the mystery of the human psyche.

This interest was deepened during Jung's years at the Burghölzli mental hospital in Zurich where the pathological variants of so-called normality fascinated him because they offered him the longed-for opportunity to obtain a deeper insight into the psyche in general. In psychiatry Jung realized that paranoid ideas and hallucinations contain a germ of meaning and that a personality, a life history, a pattern of hopes and desires lie behind the psychosis. Patients may appear dull and apathetic, or totally imbecilic, but more is going on in their minds that is meaningful than appearances suggest. The same sense of mystery and awe which Jung experienced so profoundly in his childhood remained with him during his work with the insane. Jung was convinced that each patient held a secret, a story within a hidden personality. This attitude in Jung, this level of sensitivity to the mystery of life itself, is the mark of a mystic, for the truly spiritual person is sensitive to meaning everywhere, especially where others are least likely to look for it.

One might call Jung a mystic because, like individuals of the spirit from biblical times onward, he was attuned to the meaning of dreams. Indeed, some of Jung's earliest dreams dating back to his childhood profoundly influenced the course of his life. Jung acknowledged the dream as something "given," an irrational fact with hidden meaning to be discovered through personal reflection and the search for analogous images in the history of culture. Jung's dreams were often the clues to his most profound speculative insights. His theory of the collective unconscious was intimately related to the following dream:

> I was in a house I did not know, which had two stories. It was "my house." I found myself in the upper story, where there was a kind of salon furnished with fine old pieces in rococco style. On the walls hung a number of precious old paintings. I wondered that this should be my house, and thought, "Not bad." But then it occurred to me that I did not know what the lower floor looked like. Descending the stairs, I reached the ground floor. There everything was much older, and I realized that this part of the house must date from about the fifteenth or sixteenth century. The furnishings were medieval; the floors were of red brick. Everywhere it was rather dark. I went from one room to another, thinking, "Now I really must explore the whole house." I came upon a heavy door, and opened it. Beyond it, I discovered a stone stairway that led down into the cellar. Descending again, I found myself in a beautifully vaulted room which looked exceedingly ancient. Examining the walls, I discovered layers of brick among the ordinary stone blocks, and chips of brick in the mortar. As soon as I saw this I knew that the walls dated from Roman times. My interest now was intense. I looked more closely at the floor. It was of stone slabs, and in one of

these I discovered a ring. When I pulled it,
the stone slab lifted, and again I saw a stair-
way of narrow stone steps leading down into
the depths. These, too, I descended, and
entered a low cave cut into the rock. Thick
dust lay on the floor, and in the dust were
scattered bones and broken pottery, like
remains of a primitive culture. I discovered
two human skulls, obviously very old and
half disintegrated. Then I awoke.[3]

In interpreting this dream, Jung saw that the house represented
a kind of image of the psyche, of his state of consciousness at the time
with hitherto unconscious additions. Consciousness was represented
by the salon. The ground level stood for the first level of unconsciousness, and the deeper he went, the more alien and darker the scene
became until in the cave he discovered remains of the primitive
culture, that is, the world of the primitive within himself. This
primitive psyche borders on the life of the animal soul. The dream
pointed out further reaches to consciousness: the long uninhabited
ground floor in medieval style, then the Roman cellar, and finally the
prehistoric cave—all of these images signified past times and passed
stages of consciousness. Jung felt his dream pointed to the foundations
of cultural history—a history of successive layers of consciousness—and postulated something of an impersonal nature underlying the psyche. This interpretation "clicked" for him, and the
dream became a guiding image because it was his first inkling of a
collective *a priori* beneath the personal psyche. This dream too,
marked Jung's departure from Freud's interpretation of dreams as
pointing to hidden contents relating exclusively to the personal life.

Another source of Jung's ineffable knowledge was his awareness
of a number two personality. He recounts of his boyhood that

somewhere deep in the background he always knew that he was two persons: one was the son of his parents, who went to school and was less intelligent and attentive, less hard-working and decent, and less clean than many other boys. The other was grown up—old, in fact—skeptical, mistrustful, remote from the human world, but close to nature, the earth, the sun, the moon, the weather, all living creatures, and above all close to the night, to dreams, and to whatever God worked directly in him. Nature seemed, like himself, to have been set aside by God as non-divine, although created by Him as an expression of Himself. Nothing could persuade him that "in the image of God" applied only to human beings. The high mountains, the rivers, lakes, trees, flowers, and animals seemed far better to exemplify the essence of God than people with their ridiculous clothes, their meanness, vanity, mendacity, and abhorrent egotism— all qualities with which Jung was only too familiar from himself, that is, from personality number one, the schoolboy of 1890. Besides this world existed another realm, like a temple in which anyone who entered was transformed and suddenly overpowered by a vision of the whole cosmos, so that one could only marvel and admire, forgetful of oneself. Here lived the "Other," who knew God as a hidden, personal, and at the same time suprapersonal secret. Here nothing separated the individual from God: indeed, the human mind seemed to look down upon Creation simultaneously with God.[4]

This profound revelation of Jung's inner experience described in his autobiography speaks for itself. Throughout his life, personality number two always existed, the mystical side of himself complementing his outer life. During the period of Jung's confrontation with the unconscious, the image of his number two personality emerged as Philemon, the wise old man of antiquity, who along with a host of other figures, assailed his consciousness. Jung spent a lifetime unravelling these mysteries.

Jung's second home, Bollingen, the tower he constructed on

upper Lake Zurich, was an expression of his number two personality. Here the spontaneous images given to him were painted on the walls and carved in stone throughout the house and garden. Here the trees, springs, plants, and animals, as well as an inner private room reserved only for meditation, were the environment which nourished his mystical nature.

Jung's mysticism also manifested itself in his attitude toward religion. Although reared a Christian in a family with clergymen on both sides, Jung did not approach religion from a theological standpoint. Instead, he began with the immediacy of his awareness of the ineffable, his sense of the presence of the "Other," and from this mystical side he looked to the images in all religions for meaning. He found fundamental differences in forms of awareness and in intellectual conceptions not only between East and West, but also between different periods of time and epochs of cultural history. Yet in the images of all religions ancient and modern he found the same fundamental structures: unity, plurality, duality, trinity, quaternity, quintessence. In specific images of particular religions, namely, rituals, mythologies, and dogmas, he found expressions of primoridal powers. His theory of the archetypes provided a theoretical explanation of the primordial patterns found in all religions.

Jung also stressed the fundamental difference in religious attitudes East and West: the Eastern mind being more preoccupied with a Universal Self, while Western religions incorporate a more personal relationship to the divine. While both forms of religious experience are authentic, Jung stressed the necessity for the Western mind to preserve its need for personal relatedness. He held that no relation to the inner self occurs without relation to an other. This tenet underlies his whole theory of the psychology of transference, considered to be essential in the development of personality.

When asked in a personal interview whether he believed in God, Jung answered, "I do not belive, I know."[5] This statement made in Jung's later years represents the culmination of his religious development beginning with the early inner contradictions he experienced in relation to Christian teachings, through the intensely scientific orientation of his thought during his youth and student years and the subsequent influence of Freud's negative outlook toward religion, and finally through his later penetrating studies of world myths and religions. The chronological development of Jung's religious ideas as expressed in his writings has been documented in scholarly detail.[6] Of more concern, however, to a consideration of Jung's mysticism is his personal attitude in regard to the question of God. From his later writings, particularly, "Answer to Job,"[7] one sees that Jung was profoundly aware of the mystery at the core of religion: the problem of good and evil in relation to the ultimate meaning of reality. Jung experienced acutely this enigma, having witnessed the devastation of two world wars. In his personal life, however, he did discover meaning and purpose. His own myth carries a commitment to human consciousness and morality vis-à-vis the mystery of human existence. Having lived his myth in his own life, his intuitions about purpose and destiny were verified. Hence, he could say, "I do not believe, I know."

Jung also found meaning and divine intervention in every incident in his life which went contrary to normal plans and expectations. He lived with a sense of inner direction, yet with an openness leading often through contradictions to a specific way.

One could say that Jung's mystical side led to his theory of synchronicity, for had he himself not experienced the atemporal, ubiquitous dimensions of the psyche, as in his early experience with spiritualistic phenomena, including the subsequent careful observations of occult experiments which expanded his view of the human psyche, he may not have been drawn so intimately into the psychophysical realm. Jung's life was filled with synchronistic occurrences, and while these "facts" were intimately woven into the personal sphere, he felt the need to integrate them into a theoretical framework.

Consequently, he was profoundly interested in J.B. Rhine's experiments in extra-sensory perception at Duke University.[8] These experiments along with numerous other cases of spontaneous fore-knowledge, non-spatial perceptions, psychokinesis, etc., were the empirical data supporting his theory of synchronicity with the implied metaphysics of a psychophysical universe. However, Jung's own mystical side and the experiences of synchronistic events in his own life were primarily the starting point for his theory of the relativization of time and space in the human psyche. These experiences supported his view on life after death as well. He wrote, "Not only my own dreams but occasionally the dreams of others, helped me to shape, revise, or confirm my views on a life after death."[9]

Jung's view was that the limitation of consciousness in space and time is such an overwhelming reality that every occasion when this fundamental truth is broken through must rank as an event of the highest theoretical significance, for it would prove that the space-time barrier can be annulled. He stated that under certain conditions, the psyche because of a quality essential to it, namely, its relatively trans-spatial and trans-temporal nature, can break through the barriers of space and time. This possible transcendence of space-time, for which a good deal of evidence exists, suggests the possibility of a form of existence without space and time. Jung held that this hypothetical possibility presents a scientific question mark that merits serious consideration for a long time to come. He believed that since the nature of the psyche reaches into obscurities far beyond the scope of understanding, one might well listen to the needs of one's heart or the ancient lessons of human wisdom and draw the conclusion that the psyche, in its deepest reaches, participates in a form of existence beyond space and time, and thus partakes of what is inadequately and symbolically described as "eternity." He added that anyone who does not draw this conclusion whether from skepticism, rebellion against tradition, lack of courage, inadequate psychological experience, or thoughtless ignorance, stands very little chance, statistically, of becoming a pioneer of the mind, but has instead the indubitable certainty of coming into conflict with the truths of one's blood. Whether these are absolute truths one cannot determine; nevertheless, Jung maintained, they conform with the deepest human instincts, denial of which results in uprootedness, disorientation, and meaningless.[10]

In regard to life after death, Jung believed that this dimension is intimately bound up with the temporal dimension, for if a conscious existence occurs after death, cognition is dependent on what is known before death and on the level of consciousness attained by humanity in time. He felt that the unlimited knowledge which seems to be present in nature can be comprehended only when the time is ripe for it. Since he believed that omniscience or omni-consciousness is at the disposal only of the living, the maximum awareness which has been attained anywhere forms the upper limit of knowledge to which the dead can attain. This is the reason why Jung held earthly life to be of such significance.[11]

These beliefs of Jung spring from his inner experience, his mystical nature, as well as from his long experience as a psychotherapist. In observing a great many people as they approached death, he found in their images of the unconscious, rebirth symbols such as changes of locality, journeys, and the like, which frequently extended in a dream series for over a year. He was astonished to see how little ado the unconscious psyche makes of death, as though death were something relatively unimportant. However, the unconscious, Jung said, seems all the more interested in how one dies; that is, whether the attitude of consciousness is adjusted to dying or not.[12] The collective psyche expressed in all the great religions of the world regards death as the fulfillment of life's meaning and as its goal in the truest sense. The unconscious of the individual who is in touch with the deepest instincts prepares one for this final moment.

Regarding the theory of karma and reincarnation, Jung found it acceptable only as psychic heredity in the very widest sense of the word, that is, as the inheritance of psychic characteristics. He held that essential phenomena of life express themselves in the main psychically, just as other inherited characteristics express themselves in the main physiologically on the physical level. Among these inherited psychic factors is a special class not confined to family or race, the universal dispositions of the mind analogous to Plato's Forms. The forms, however, for Jung are not confined to categories of reason, but include categories of the imagination as well. These eternally inherited forms have no specific content in themselves, but appear as specific only in the course of an individual's life when personal experience is taken up precisely in them.[13] Jung held, however, that so far as he knew no inheritance of individual pre-natal, or pre-uterine, memories occurs. He saw all spiritualistic literature concerning communications from the "spirit world" as emanating from the archetypal contents of the unconscious, partly through the medium's establishing contact with the spirit world. Consequently, these data he regarded as psychic facts rather than as physical or metaphysical realities.[14]

Was Jung a mystic? Yes, he was a mystic, but not *only* a mystic. He was also an empiricist in the broadest sense of the term. His mystical insights meant nothing to him unless they could be verified with the data of history and contemporary research. This combination of profound intuitive insight with rigorous attention to external facts, along with fidelity to a sense of destiny and purpose, is the essence of Jung's genius. It is also, in the most complete sense, the mark of a genuine philosopher.

CHAPTER 10

All references to C. G. Jung's works, unless otherwise indicated, are taken from the *Collected Works* (C. W.) second edition, 20 vols., Princeton University Press.

1. C. G. Jung, *Memories, Dreams, Reflections,* recorded and edited by Aniela Jaffé, translated from the German by Richard and Clara Winston (New York: Vintage Books, 1963) p. 20.

2. *Ibid.* 10 -107.

3. *Ibid.* 158-159.

4. *Ibid.* 44-45.

5. BBC film, "The Story of C. G. Jung."

6. James W. Heisig, *Imago Dei: A Study of C. G. Jung's Psychology of Religion* (Lewisburg, Pa.: Bucknell University Press; London: Associated University Presses, 1979).

7. "Answer to Job" (1956), C. W., 11:359-470 (553-758).

8. J. B. Rhine, *Extra-Sensory Perception* (Boston, 1934).

9. *Memories, Dreams, Reflections,* 305.

10. "The Soul and Death" (1945), C. W., 8:414-415 (815).

11. *Memories, Dreams, Reflections,* 311.

12. "The Soul and Death," *op. cit.,* 410-411 (809).

13. "Psychological Commentary on the Tibetan Book of the Dead" (1955), C. W., 11:517-519 (845).

14. *Ibid.* 525 (857).

CHAPTER 11

STAGES IN THE CREATIVE PROCESS:

The Seven Days of Creation

C. G. Jung's philosophy of creativity can be applied to the creation of a work of art and also to the creative life. As Jung said, "If you have nothing to create, then you create yourself." While Jung's theory of individuation (his philosophy of creativity applied to life) is the basis of a therapy for dealing with neurosis, it also applies to the fully lived life, one which engages the individual in the development of different facets of the personality so that the individual fulfills one's function as a highly differentiated human being and thus discovers the meaning of one's existence. The essential elements of Jung's theory involve both a sensitivity to the irrational facts of experience, such as images of the unconscious and outer events, as well as an accommodation of these facts though synthesis with the rational side of the personality. This process culminates ultimately in changes of attitude and appropriate action. Finally, through reflection one discovers the meaning of the life process for oneself. For Jung, a balance must occur between life and meaning; otherwise, one might live either an unreflective life or a too symbolic life. Suggestions of life's meaning can be discovered through myths wherein earliest records of human conscious life are manifested.

Creation myths, stories about how the world began, stem from the human psyche. In these stories, one can also discover the beginning of human awareness. Myths of creation viewed in this light are symbolic records of the dawn of human consciousness, and their unfolding symbolism can be studied as the unfolding of human awareness on many different levels. I will use Jung's theory of creativity and individuation as an instrument of analysis in unrav-

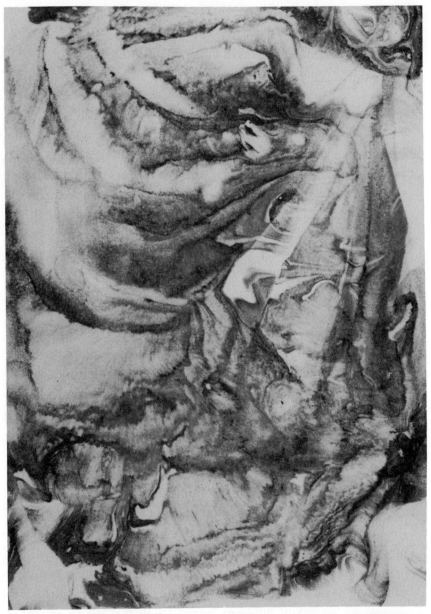

146

Lorraine Fink

Let there be light

elling meaning possibilities in the imagery of the Seven Days of Creation in the Genesis myth.

From the perspective of Jung's theory, the Seven Days may be seen as images of the ongoing development of consciousness throughout the total life process. The striking imagery of each day suggests possibilities for self-discovery as well as offers enlightenment about human engagement in the ongoing creation. Each day suggests a stage in the creative life. Jung's theory is especially applicable to Western consciousness with its traditional emphasis on the development of ego and will in the attainment of self-knowledge. Thus the affirmations of the God-image on each day of the myth can be understood as the imperative of the Self leading the individual ego through a developing awareness to the fulfillment of the highest creative potentiality and ultimately to wisdom or knowledge of the self.

THE FIRST DAY

In the beginning God created the heavens and the earth. The earth was without form and void, and darkness was upon the face of the deep; and the Spirit of God was moving over the face of the waters. And God said, "Let there be light"; and there was light. And God saw that the light was good; and God separated the light from the darkness. God called the light Day, and the darkness he called Night. And there was evening and there was morning one day. Genesis 1:1-5[1]

The first day begins with God. As an *Imago Dei,* God in the myth is a human image of what is highest and first in the human psyche. From this ultimate principle all else springs. The image presents God as dynamic: God creating the heavens and the earth; the Spirit of God moving; God saying, "Let there be light." These images suggest the essential dynamics of the human psyche: the excess energy or libido which can bring forth something new in the real sense of the word, for against this energy is chaos. God as an image of the highest principle in the human psyche is thus essentially dynamic, creative, and expansive; but that is not all—this principle is also discriminating, for it separates, and it is moral, for it values what it creates by affirming it to be good.

On the very first day, we are confronted with duality; the one and the many, or the one and the other. Without duality or separation the essential dynamism of the one cannot be manifested. Hence all philosophies and religions are immediately confronted with the problem of the one and the many. The myth begins with God, the One, and the dynamic aspect of God, the Spirit of God moving. This duality is expressed in the Brahmin and Atman of Indian philosophy, in the One and the emanations of the One in Plotinus, the Father and Son of Christianity, the higher self and the hither self of William James, and so on. In more immediate terms, it reflects the capabilities for action and respose in the human entity.

Before light, there is darkness and the deep, a void, a lack of form. These images suggest potentiality, but no beginning occurs until the Spirit of God moves over the face of the deep. An individual is unconscious and the human world does not begin until that highest principle stirs and moves over the face of one's unconsciousness, the deep. The face (a face has features) suggests what is below the surface. All movement immediately stirs the unconscious and life possibilities.

This initial stage of the creative process is a stage of inspiration, a pleasant experience when the energies are touched and the surface of life loses its stagnation and no deep disturbing currents are revealed. This is only a beginning, an initial stage that does not go anywhere—yet.

Still, it is the face of the *deep*. The unfathomable, the deep, is touched ever so lightly; yet it is touched. The deep exists and its power and potentiality will have to be brought forth if the process is to go on. This realization may bring fear: what will come forth? can I handle it? do I want it? is it better to stop now before anything gets going? Hence, for some, this is where creativity stops, inspiration dies, and one moves back to stagnation, darkness, and chaos.

By contrast, in the creation of visionary art, Jung speaks of a force in the artist that accomplishes its aims even without the conscious motivations of the artist. Here the individual is identified with the creative archetype which uses one as a vehicle through which the work of art comes into being. In this case, the imperative of the creative dynamic rules the artist during the creative process.[2] In individuation, however, each stage of the process of growing consciousness has a moral dimension. The individual must be willing to cooperate with the inspirations of the Self.[3]

For the creative process of individuation to go on, an affirmation of will is necessary. "And God said, 'Let there be light'." This is a command and also a choice to go beyond darkness and chaos. Furthermore, the *voice* in the myth calls for light. Sound comes first, then sight through light. Speech comes before understanding (light). "In the beginning was the Word" (John I). The imagery suggests that human creativity and enlightenment are dependent upon sensitivity to the imperative "Let there be light." One cannot be forced out of darkness, for one is essentially a duality. All creativity, all movement forward in the human world is dependent upon the transcendence of this duality. Individuation as a creative process involves a conscious decision. In addition to the gift of inspiration, motivation and choice are necessary.

The myth continues, "and there was light." Something results.

First occurs desire, the Spirit of God moving; then a decision, an imperative, "Let there be light"; then a result: light. "And God saw that it was good." The imagery suggests moral integrity in the most profound sense—goodness. To decide to light up one's chaos with the gift of light is a rational decision which brings about a result (light) and it is good (it feels good and right) thus far.

This is a crucial moment in the creative process. After overcoming the initial fear of the deep and its unfathomable potential, and after the conscious decision to continue the process with, "Let there be light," an immediate result occurs: light appears and it is good. So far, so good. One has experienced a moment of transcendence, a confirmation of one's act of faith in the life process.

What are the implications of this initial stage of the creative process? One must realize that for some individuals the creative process never gets started. For whatever reason, some people cannot energize the unity of consciousness to separate themselves from the chaos. They stay in unconsciousness and darkness, living in an instinctual and collective plane, like the rest of nature. Human beings are the only creatures who have the potentiality to go beyond the demands of nature, to create in another realm, to bring forth something new in the realm of culture born of the creative imagination. This consideration is not meant to disparage nature but to suggest that creativity grows out of nature, as Jung says, as a tree whose roots lie in the living being.

Significant in Genesis is the fact that human creativity does not simply happen; nature does not compel it. In some individuals the creative impulse is so strong that it dominates an entire life. But, nevertheless, the creative product is not produced naturally. In any creative works as in the creative life discrimination is necessary; conscious choices have to be made as the work progresses. Therefore, at the outset as Jung indicates, creativity, while a natural impulse found in all human beings, is more of a dormant potentiality than a dominant instinct, as, for example, the instincts of hunger and sexuality.

Creativity in the rudimentary sense, then, is selective. Not everyone will have the power, the force of will, to take a stand against the chaos and the darkness. Why? Perhaps the key to unravelling the mystery lies in the words, "and the spirit of God was moving over the face of the deep." The spirit is the creative spirit in human beings. Why does it move in some and not others? Or, does it move in everyone as a fundamental human potentiality? Surely, it does, but in human beings as in nature not all potentialities are actualized. Tremendous waste exists in nature. A heirarchy exists. We can cultivate nature as well as produce an artificial environment so that things can grow, but even then not all possibilities will be realized.

The spirit of God, or the creative spirit, is an intangible "given" in an individual which one either recognizes and cultivates and allows a voice in one's life, or in unconsciousness ignores and neglects it. However, human beings could be trained to be sensitive to this dimension in themselves, but in the last analysis, they cannot be forced to cultivate it because cultivation is dependent upon the will which is the exclusive power of the individual. The will is free.

Not only does the will belong to the individual as one's exclusive priority, but it also carries with it the responsibility of its affirmations, which could be another reason why individuals do not exercise its power. Therefore, to utter the words, "Let there be light," implies the necessity, the responsibility, to look and see. To see is the metaphor for knowing. Many people would rather not know what creative possibilites lie ahead because that would force considerations which could be upsetting. "Don't tell me about it; I would rather not know" is a familiar phrase. One can choose, then, by virtue of a negative attitude to stay in darkness and chaos. Out of fear, laziness, or stubborn ignorance, one can elect to be uncreative, unproductive, and ineffective in life. One can refuse to exercise freedom and thereby avoid the consequent responsibility of a creative life.

When we look at the metaphor of birth, a baby's cry, it's sound, is the first sign of life. The baby opens its eyes and sees the light only hours or days later. Sound comes before light and sight. The beginning of life is not easy. Separation from the womb, from the darkness where all physical needs are met, is traumatic. Psychologically, some individuals would prefer to stay in the womb, in unconsciousness and darkness, and have all needs taken care of. I suggest that the initial stage of creativity is like being born. Everything is new and different, and difficult. But, at the same time, what is highest in oneself knows that it is good.

The myth continues, "And God separated the light from the darkness": again duality, separation, discrimination. "God called the light Day, and the darkness he called Night": day consciousness, against night unconsciousness. "And there was evening and there was morning one day." Creativity begins in the evening, in the night, in the unconscious (we have to sleep on it first), before the morning of light. This separation of day and night and the acknowledgement of the first day marks the beginning of time in the human world. No time in the human sense exists in the unconscious, in darkness. Human creativity needs time; it can only happen in time, for time is the first human creation. Without time, without the isolation of one moment of consciousness, one moment of light, the human world could not exist. And when time runs out, so does the human world. Jung holds that even the dead can only know what is known in time. In the unconscious, all is known potentially, all is there, but it can only be known through human beings in time. Humanity's contribution to the ongoing creation and to collective consciousness must be made in time.

154

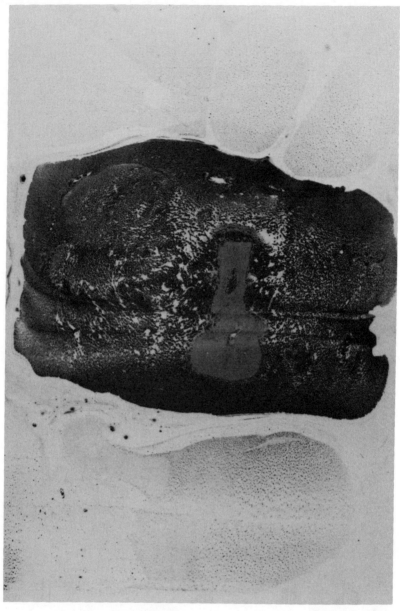

Let there be a firmament in the
    midst of the waters

Lorraine Fink

THE SECOND DAY

> And God said, "Let there be a firmament in
> the midst of the waters, and let it separate
> the waters from the waters." And God made
> the firmament and separated the waters
> which were under the firmament from the
> waters which were above the firmament.
> And it was so. And God call the firmament
> Heaven. And there was evening and there
> was morning a second day. Genesis 1:6-8.

On the first day, light was made and the first duality in creation, light and darkness, came into being symbolizing the dawn of
consciousness and the first stage of the creative process. With light,
a second duality follows: the separation of the waters as higher and
lower and the establishment of a firmament (heaven) in between.
Light has made possible a differentiation of potentialities in life
symbolized by the separation of the waters from the vantage point of
the firmament in between. The creative spirit, symbolized by "and
God said," has provided a perspective, a firmament, from which one
can contemplate the range of life's possibilities, as higher and lower.
This is still an initial discriminatory stage in the creative process; it
follows upon the decision to ask and receive illumination: "let there
be light; and there was light."

The creative spirit seeks that which is new. The firmament,
therefore, is necessary, for without this realm would be no possibility of human consciousness stepping outside of nature, so to speak,
thus transcending nature and unconsciousness, and thereby consciously participating in the ongoing creation. The firmament is
necessary in order to separate the waters: "Let there be a firmament
in the midst of the waters, and let it separate the waters from the

waters." Discrimination (separation) is only possible from a different perspective. In the purely natural (instinctual) realm, nature takes its course. The laws of nature prevail. All is unconscious and compulsory. The firmament, then, is that *other* ground or perspective which the creative spirit provides. This perspective would not be possible without the initial illumination provided by the creative spirit: "Let there be light." The firmament as heaven suggests an *ideal* vantage point beyond nature which is provided so that humanity might transcend nature in the creation of the human world. Heaven does not belong to human beings but to God; yet an individual is given a moment of heaven, a bit of heaven, a glimpse of the divine, at the beginning of the creative process.

Once the firmament has been provided making discrimination possible what meaning is suggested in the images of the higher and lower waters?

The lower waters are the waters of life itself: nature, the seas and lakes, rivers and streams teaming with life in its varied forms. The lower waters are also the waters of the body: the uterine water, the spinal and seminal fluids, urine and perspiration. All of these waters of nature flow uninterruptedly. They belong to life in its inexorable course. They flow on the unconsciousness of nature.

"The waters from above" suggest images of rain, dew, vapors, waterfalls, fountains, distilled water, baptismal waters, tears, drinking water, and holy waters used in ritual cleansings. Waters from above carry neither life nor the potentials and wastes of life. Waters from above purify, fructify, nourish, and cleanse. Waters from above satisfy the thirst of humanity and earth. This water cleans the air and body, heals and beautifies. Without rain and drinking water, the earth dries up and no longer yields its fruits while the body is parched with thirst and slowly dies. Without tears, the soul dries up also—with no affect, no inspiration, no laughter or joy, no love—for tears are the waters of the soul. Tears flow from the emotions, that middle ground in an individual between the conscious and the unconscious.

Jung says that without affect, emotion, the psychic energy necessary for the images of the unconscious to reach consciousness is lacking. After the waters of the soul that have been dammed up are released, tears flow. Tears come when one is truly touched, when the affect is finally released. Tears may be held back through training and self-discipline, but eventually the soul must cleanse itself of its fullness, excesses, and wastes. Plato speaks of one form of divine madness as stemming from what he calls, "too much soul."[4] Tears can come with too much soul, but likewise the lack of tears can indicate too little soul. The waters from above are necessary for all that is higher in human life, for all that belongs exclusively to the human world.

Thus far, the imagery of the second day of creation suggests that from the ideal perspective of the firmament one can discern two distinct levels of human existence: one in which nature flows indiscriminately and without purpose beyond life itself, and the other in which life is purified and made better through nurture, cleansings, cultivation, rituals, and respect for the emotions. On the one hand, the lower waters suggest the undifferentiated swamp of life's potentialities, while on the other hand the upper waters nourish the higher human life manifested in civilization and culture.

The waters from above, while in one sense given, as rain and spontaneous tears, in another sense they may be deliberately cultivated through rituals and purification methods. Rituals exist for rainmaking in primitive cultures, and in more advanced civilization rituals exist for tears, as Aristotle notes in the *Poetics* that the purpose of tragedy is to cleanse and purge the emotions. Poetry, art, and music cultivate and call forth the waters of the soul, while the purified life cultivates nature rather than exploits it.

The waters from above, then, nourish the higher life while the waters from below sustain life from the purely natural standpoint. Both are necessary for human existence. The waters from above coincide with civilization and culture in its purest form, and only from this perspective can the firmament, from which vantage point came the initial discrimination, be called Heaven. Heaven, therefore, symbolizes that ideal which is necessary for human beings to rise above nature and unconsciousness. The vision of the heavenly city in an indelible image in the human psyche attesting to human consent and ascent to a higher vision of life and the calling forth of something new. This ideal order of reality has been symbolically projected as the New Jerusalem, the Kindgom of Heaven, Plato's Republic, Augustine's City of God, Dante's Paradiso, More's Utopia, and is the unconscious ideal of every optimistic political system.

What, then, does all this mean in terms of the creative process? The imagery suggests that creativity involves a continual refining of movement and direction from a standpoint provided by an initial intuitive spark or light. At first, the stance is only a point of separation, but after the separation the stance becomes a superior vantage point (heaven), an ideal toward which the whole process is directed. Susanne Langer states that the first word, or line, or tone, or stroke of the brush determines the entire work of art. That initial step impelled by the creative spirit is the impetus which establishes the work as a whole.[5] This principle can be understood more simply in Zen calligraphy. Likewise, in a human life, that first glimpse of one's own metaphor establishes the ground of an entire spiritual journey— at least up to the point where the journey is complete and the metaphor fulfilled. Another life, another metaphor, another journey is something else.

And what is the meaning of the waters? The waters suggest the potentialities of spirit and nature. From the Jungian standpoint, the tension of spirit and nature must be sustained. To give oneself over entirely to either side is to lose the dynamics of life in the world in the most complete sense. Jung warns against one-sidedness: all spirit or all nature. The individual tension from one's unique firmament sustains the creative work and the creative life. Both the waters from above and the waters from below are necessary for the fully lived life and for the fully developed work of art or culture. Without water there is no life, no nourishment of body and soul.

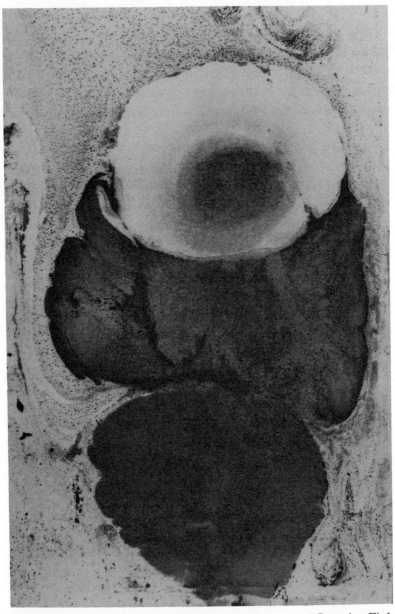

Let the earth put forth
vegetation, plants yielding seed

Lorraine Fink

THE THIRD DAY

And God said, "Let the waters under the
heavens be gathered together into one place,
and let the dry land appear". And it was so.
God called the dry land Earth, and the
waters that were gathered together he called
Seas. And God saw that it was good. And
God said, "Let the earth put forth vegetation,
plants yielding seed, and fruit trees bearing
fruit in which is their seed, each according to
its kind, upon the earth". And it was so. The
earth brought forth vegetation, plants yielding seed according to their own kinds, and
trees bearing fruit in which is their seed,
each according to its kind. And God saw that
it was good. And there was evening and
there was morning, a third day.
Genesis 1:9-13

On the third day, dry land appears. "Let the waters under the
heavens be gathered into place." These are the lower waters. In the
realm of the lower waters, a further division in the creative process
takes place: the emergence of land from the waters and the separation of earth and seas. "And God saw that it was good." In the
creative process, the work or the creative life must be accomplished
through the life potentialities of the lower waters (nature). When dry
land appears out of the lower waters, this is a moment of decision
"Let the dry appear"; the indiscriminate flow of nature (the lower
waters) is stopped, so to speak, and transformed to another domain
(dry land) from which different fruits of nature can be yielded. No
plants and trees can appear from the waters alone. So the emergence

of earth from the waters symbolizes a conscious rational choice to change something in life: to gather the potentialities and energies that have been hitherto undirected and thereby make possible a new dimension with fruits thereof. Without the emergence of land, through the conscious decision to let it appear, the creative process could have gone no further. Once this step has been taken, however, a new realm exists and it feels right: "And God saw that it was good." So far so good. One can take only one step at a time.

Notice that creation is not just change. It is transformation. Following transformation, new possibilities come to exist. Before the act of transformation, these creative possibilities could not even be imagined. They were not a reality. Trees and fruits were not possible before. This is an important message for the creative life. Until one takes the next necessary step with full consciousness and will, one cannot yet fathom what possibilities lie ahead.

The creative life, according to Jung, is the conscious moral life. To live in unconsciousness and close to nature may be fine for earlier stages of human development, but for the mature individual on the path of individuation, in Jung's sense, the imperative exists that one continue to move toward more refined levels of consciousness and morality. However, the individual can take only one step at a time.

Once the dry land appears, however, further differentation is possible. "Let the earth put forth vegetation, plants yielding seeds, and fruit trees bearing fruit in which is their seed." Up to this point, all had been fluid: the chaos, the waters, the spirit of God moving. The firmament as an ideal (heaven) existed, yes, but nothing more could be said about it because it is not in the realm of human actuality. It is above and beyond. The phrase, "And God saw that it was good" is missing on the second day. We cannot live in the ideal, in heaven. We can only create in time. However, with the establishment of dry land, earth, is the beginning of *continuity:* plants yielding seeds and trees bearing fruit with their seeds can now be sustained.

This represents a tremendous step forward in the evolution of the human psyche. Culture can only develop with continuity from one generation to the next. The creative life does not happen in a day. In the creative life, are beginnings which bear fruit, and the fruits in turn have their seeds. The fruits of the creative life are ongoing; they reproduce their kind. This suggests that the creative life is one of leadership—either directly or indirectly—fruits and seeds supplying one generation to the next.

As long as the movement of life is fluid with no dry land, no establishment of the human world can occur, no sustained consciousness and no ongoing development of the fruits of consciousness. Notice now what the dry land yields: vegetation, plants yielding seed, and fruit trees bearing fruit which contain their seed. Vegetation, plants—the most elementary life—the creative life starts here. Life does not begin with higher forms and descend to the lower. It begins simply with plants. What does this mean for the human psyche? This image suggests that the creative life, following the initial illumination and first steps of discrimination, establishes a ground from which it can grow simply at first, with plants yielding seeds, that is, with simple projects having continuity, and then with larger projects, trees bearing fruits which contain seeds. Once a ground has been established from which one can grow, then new life takes form, a life which has continuity and bears fruit with still further continuity. This feels good. In reaching this point in one's development, one has arrived at the third day.

In the creative life, one can stop here, stop with one's work and the fruit of one's labors. One can have a following. Is it not enough to rise up out of the swamp of unconsciousness, to see one's ideal and one's possibilities, to establish a dry ground, some stability in life, and to yield something nourishing to others that continues to sustain itself as a source of ongoing life and fulfillment? Yes, it is enough for some people. On the natural level, one can make something of one's life in the world. One can have a profession or marry, live a good life, and have progeny either on the biological level (children and grandchildren) or on the professional level (doing work and making a mark in the world).

This is a stage of accomplishment which in Jungian terms could be called the accomplishments of the first half of life. The higher self (God) finds it good. Jung holds that the task of the first half of life is to ground oneself in the world. One has to begin with a place (dry land). One has to settle down, stop the flow, so to speak, in order to be fully conscious initially. Without this initial break in the flow of experience, no beginning, no sustained effort over time could occur. What is needed, therefore, is to mark time in the human world so that creative efforts can develop (the earth can put forth vegetation) and have continuity (plants yielding seeds) to facilitate larger efforts with ongoing results (trees bearing fruit which contain their seed) that are varied and multiple. And all of this brings a fulfillment according to the direction of the higher Self (and God saw that it was good).

"And there was evening and there was morning a third day"—a stage of life is brought to a close. When something is finished it is finished. For some people this is enough, and the germ of personality (to use Jung's terminology) does not offer the possibility of anything more. One has filled the cup to the brim. But for others more remains; the second half of life.

166

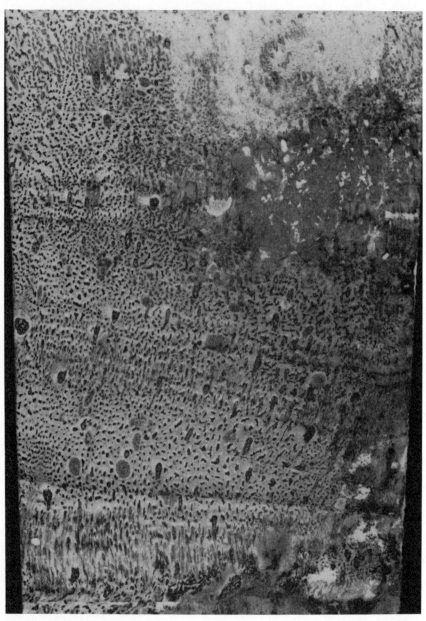

Let there be lights in
  the firmament of the heavens

Lorraine Fink

THE FOURTH DAY

And God said, "let there be lights in the
firmament of the heavens to separate the
day from the night; and let them be for signs
and for seasons and days and years, and let
them be lights in the firmament of the heavens to give light upon the earth". And it was
so. And God made the two great lights, the
greater light to rule the day, and the lesser
light to rule the night: he made the stars also.
And God set them in the firmament of the
heavens to give light upon the earth, to rule
over the day and over the night, and to
separate the light from the darkness. And
God saw that it was good. And there was
evening and there was morning, a fourth
day.
Genesis 1:14-19

On the second day, the firmament was established separating
the upper and lower waters, and God called the firmament heaven.
On the fourth day, lights are created in the firmament. Up to this
point, day and night have been separated, but night is not illuminated until the fourth day. This suggests in the creative process and
the creative life an initial period when the conscious (day) and
unconscious (night) are not fully differentiated. Now we are told
something about the night and its lights. The greater light rules the
day, the world of daylight consciousness, and the lesser light rules
the night and illuminates the unconscious. This suggests that the
greater light to rule the day is the sun (in alchemy, the masculine
principle) while the lesser light to rule the night is the moon (the

feminine principle). In both worlds, there is light to see, to know: the sun to see in the day, and the moon to see in the dark.

And then the stars, "he made the stars also," suggest the differentiated luminosities of the unconscious. "And God set them in the firmament of the heavens to give light upon the earth, to rule over the day and over the night, and to separate the light from the darkness." The stars can be seen only at night. The imagery suggests that some secrets can be known only by direct illumination from the unconscious, but they also rule over the day and the night, which suggests that all seeing, *all* understanding needs the illumination of the unconscious. These lights also create order: "let them be signs for seasons and for days and years," and thereby provide a more profound sense of time. The lights of the heavens (sun, moon, and stars) rule both day and night (conscious and unconscious) and also make possible an understanding of nature: "give light upon the earth." The symbolism is reminiscent of Plato's Highest Good, in the *Republic* symbolized by the sun, which not only causes things to be but also to be known.[6]

In Western alchemy, the sun and moon symbolize masculine and feminine principles. In Japanese mythology, the images are reversed: the sun is feminine and the moon masculine. Regardless of the reversal, the images are universally seen as co-principles ruling the contra-sexual dominant of the human psyche.

On the other hand, the stars can be looked upon as the myriad archetypal energies which interpenetrate each other in the structure of the psyche. Jung speaks of the stars and the science of the stars (astrology) as a projection of the collective unconscious. He says:

> The collective unconscious—so far as we can say anything about it at all—appears to consist of mythological motifs or primordial images....In fact, the whole of mythology

could be taken as a sort of projection of the
collective unconscious. We can see this most
clearly if we look at the heavenly constella-
tions, whose originally chaotic forms were
organized through the projection of images.
This explains the influence of the stars as
asserted by astrologers. These influences are
nothing but unconscious, introspective perceptions of the activity of the collective
unconscious.[7]

Just as the archetypal energies symbolized by the sun and moon
evoke and govern the two main psychic dominants, the contra-
sexual modes of differentiation, so also the stars as archetypes
illuminate or evoke and likewise govern the myriad energies which
interpenetrate the complexity of the human psyche. The creative
individual when mature is in touch with all of these inspirations and
powers and can accommodate them in work or in life. The archetypes of the collective unconscious, symbolized by the sun, moon,
and stars, structure the human psyche and also provide the energies
(lights) whereby the images can reach consciousness. To be in touch
with these inspirations is a necessary stage in more mature and fully
developed creativity. When these insights and inspirations are both
given and accepted, another level has been achieved. And it feels
good.

We might look upon the imagery of the fourth to the sixth day of
the creation myth as a more advanced creativity, or as the second
half of life in Jung's theory of individuation. At this stage, day and night
are fully separated. In conventional language, one has achieved more
objectivity in one's perception of the world, but at the same time one
has also arrived at a more profound understanding of the deeper
realities of human existence. In Jungian terminology: a conscious-

ness of the unconscious. Initially, after the illumination of the first day, consciousness and differentiation occur only in the daylight world. Now there are lights in the firmament to light up the night so that one can see in the dark and can become conscious of the unconscious. The lights are also "for signs, for seasons, days, and years," so that one can become conscious of levels of time other than ego-time, such as the time of the archetypes: mythic time, cycles, epochs, eons, and the consciousness of non-time. And all of these levels of time can simultaneously interpenetrate each other in human awareness when consciousness is illuminated by the heavenly lights. In this diffuseness one can participate in many different times at once.

"And let them be lights in the firmament of the heavens to give light upon the earth." Cognizance of the lights of the heavens (of the luminosities which make possible the clarity of one's projections) also illumines one's understanding of earth and nature. Thus, one can cultivate nature in a more refined way. One can see everything in different lights and can thereby enhance one's creative involvement in the world. The second half of life is the life if individuation when one lives more from within, from the refinement of spirit as well as the refinement of nature. The second half of life is the life of culture when one can more fully appreciate other dimensions of time, ancient civilizations, esoteric sciences, other times and places, for a deeper understanding of the world now comes from an inner illumination.

To see the stars on the fourth day is to discover a whole new world, the world of the spirit. This world is within, yet it remains unseen and unknown until that appropriate moment in life arrives when the creative spirit permits it to be revealed. Analogously, Jung says the fourth function of the human psyche is the hardest to develop and very few people reach this stage of spiritual growth; yet through the fourth function the greatest creative energy is released.

The fourth function provides the most immediate access to the unconscious—in the myth this level of development is symbolized by the lights of the heavens on the fourth day. Notice, however, that in the myth the experience is preceded by the imperative, "Let there be lights in the firmament of the heavens." Every stage of the creative process and of spiritual development involves an affirmation of the higher Self. With this affirmation and the acceptance of new lights, one undergoes a complete transformation, and a whole new world opens, as we shall see on the fifth day.

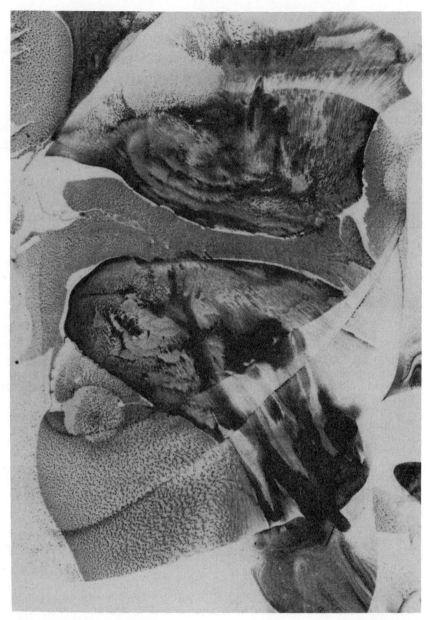

God created the great
    sea monsters

Lorraine Fink

THE FIFTH DAY

And God said, "Let the waters bring forth
swarms of living creatures, and let birds fly
above the earth across the firmament of the
heavens". So God created the great sea
monsters and every living creature that
moves, with which the waters swarm, according to their kinds, and every winged bird
according to its kind. And God saw that it was
good. And God blessed them saying, "Be
fruitful and multiply and fill the waters in
the seas, and let birds multiply on the earth".
And there was evening and there was a
morning, a fifth day.
Genesis 1:20-23

Following the second illumination, which takes place on the
fourth day when the sun, moon, and stars light up the heavens, the
birds and the great sea monsters appear on the fifth day. The
appearance earlier of plants with fruits and seeds represents one
level of creativity; birds and fish now appear to symbolize another
level. The images suggest the spiritual powers and life of the world.
The great sea monsters are symbolic of living embodiments of great
powers of the psyche; swarming waters, the fecundity of the psyche;
winged birds, the uplifting spiritual powers of the psyche. The great
lights of the heavens illumine the world in all of its richness, power,
fecundity, an uplifting grace. "All these creatures according to their
kind" suggests genera or classes (archetypal categories) of creative
endeavors that nevertheless carry a singularity, namely, *each*
according to its kind. In the creative life, the dynamics has reached a
heightened moment of fulfillment, for now life is on a higher plane,

more complex and diverse, yet still in touch with those primordial forms of the psyche.

"God saw that it was good and blessed them saying, 'Be fruitful and multiply and fill the earth." These primordial creatures, the fish and birds, are like those great works of art and culture that become the monuments and the prototypes for whole trends and styles which follow. They are also like the great heroes and leaders whom people admire and emulate. They are blessed and good and are multiplied and fill the earth.

This stage of the creative process produces great art and great people, but it only happens following the illumination from the heavens. These great individuals (great in their lives and in their work) are in touch with the heavenly lights. They see by day and night and are in touch with the wisdom of the conscious and the unconscious. They also have the illumination of the stars, the arche-types, which from the Jungian perspective are the primordial powers of the differentiated psyche. These great individual and these great works produce long-lasted results in the world. They transcend time: seasons, days and years. In Jung's sense, they could be said to live in archetypal time, for their earthly existence does not end with a physical death. The great works live on and the great individuals survive in history, myth, and legend. They are indeed blessed; they are fruitful and they multiply.

Plants belong to the earth, where human beings also live and breathe. So the creation of the plants symbolizes an earlier and more natural creativity. But fish belong to the waters and birds to the air. Birds and fish represent dimensions of life that are not easily access-ible: birds and fish have access to great heights and great depths. When these creatures are created in the myth, the symbolism sug-gests that after the fourth day, or in Jungian terms after gaining access to the fourth function, an individual has access to the fullness of one's creative powers. One can then bring forth something new which touches the great heights and depths of reality. Through the illumination of the great lights, one can now bring new heights and depths to the human world. Through one's work and life an individual can extend the boundaries of human perspective and thereby allow those who come after a vision of a new heaven and a new earth. Great works and great people represent landmarks on the frontiers of human consciousness. Without their tremendous gifts, the human world as we know it would not exist. However, although such greatness exists, it is beyond the purview and the appreciation of those who have never taken the required steps on life's journey.

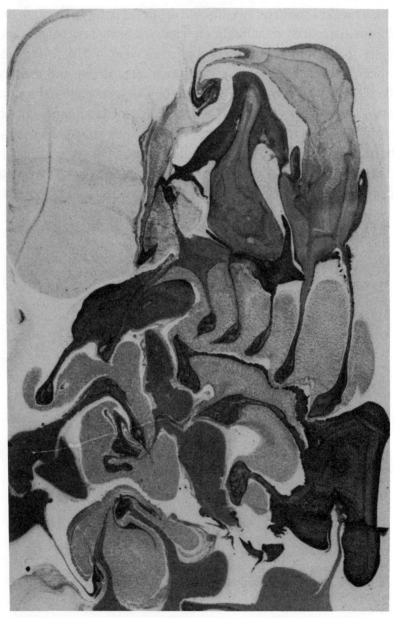

Male and female created he them   Lorraine Fink

THE SIXTH DAY

And God said, "Let the earth bring forth
living creatures according to their kinds: cattle and creeping things and beasts of the
earth according to their kind". And it was so.
And God made the beasts of the earth
according to their kind and the cattle according to their kind, and everything that creeps
upon the ground according to its kind. And
God saw that it was good. Then God said,
"Let us make man in our image, after our
likeness; and let them have dominion over
the fish of the sea, and over the birds of the
air, and over the cattle, and over all the earth,
and over every creeping thing that creeps
upon the earth." So God created man in his
own image, in the image of God he created
him; male and female he created them. And
God blessed them, and God said to them, "Be
fruitful and multiply, and fill the earth and
subdue it; and have dominion over the fish of
the sea and over the birds of the air and over
every living thing that moves upon the
earth." And God said, "Behold I have given
you every plant yielding seed which is upon
the face of all the earth, and every tree with
seed in its fruit; you shall have them for food.
And to every beast of the earth, and to every
bird of the air, and to everything that creeps
on the earth, everything that has the breath
of life, I have given every green plant for

food". And it was so. And God saw everything that he had made, and behold, it was very good. And there was evening and there was morning, a sixth day.
Genesis 1:24-31

On the sixth day, animal and human life are created. Cattle and creeping things and beasts of the earth are called forth from the earth, but human beings are created in the image and likeness of God. This imagery suggests that the creative process ultimately reflects itself and comes to know itself. It has been said that all art mirrors the self,[8] and likewise that the goal of human life is to know itself: "Let us make man in our own image and likeness." Like the God-figure of the Genesis story, an individual comes to self knowledge through creativity. Great artists may or may not know themselves through their work, but the person embarked on the path of individuation, comes to know oneself not only through living the creative life, but also by consciously reflecting upon it. However, an individual must first project an image of oneself in life and work.

In the later stages of the creative process, after the heavens light up and order the world, then the great creative results come about: the great sea monsters and the winged birds are ordered to multiply and fill the earth. The symbolism suggests the great powers of the soul—the greatness of the psyche. After this creation, the creatures of the earth next called forth are closer to human beings and are associated with human creation since they appear on the same day. The cattle and creeping things and beasts of the earth symbolize the natural part of human beings which belongs more exclusively to nature, as for example, the appetites and instincts.

But when God makes human beings in his own image and likeness, another dimension is added. They becomes God-like. At this moment of creation, they are blessed, told to be fruitful and multiply, to fill the earth and subdue it. They are given power over everything. Furthermore, when created in God's image, human beings are identified as male and female. God's image is male and female, suggesting that sexuality belongs to higher human nature, to the total character, and not simply to an animal aspect. Sexuality belongs to the image and likeness of God. Sexuality, therefore, is at the heart of reality. It has a cosmic nature, as reflected in the ancient conceptions of the sun and moon as male and female, in the primitive projection of androgynous god-figures, and in the yin and yang of Taoism.

Accompanying the masculine and feminine aspects of God are two possessions, both of which God gives to human beings, power and food. These are given after human beings are blessed and told to be fruitful and multiply. Food belongs to the feminine aspect, which is shared with all of nature, for the food is given to all the creatures of the earth, but the power, the masculine aspect, is given only to human beings. They are told to fill the earth and subdue it, to have dominion over the fish, over the birds, and over every living thing. Food belongs to the nurturing side of human nature that preserves life; power belongs to the governing side which creates order. Here an injunction for the highest creativity is called forth: human beings are told to take charge.

To "fill the earth and subdue it" demands both the feminine and the masculine sides of human nature: the capabilities both to nurture and govern. Neither one without the other will do: nurture alone leads to indiscriminate life and eventually back to the swamp and chaos, while order alone leads to the extinction of life. When human beings realize their highest imperative, that they must take charge and both nurture and govern, they are given a final challenge, and the tension of their innate duality as masculine and feminine must be both preserved and transcended. That tension must be preserved in the recognition that both sides of human existence, nurturing and governing, are necessary, but it must be transcended through the creation of a civilization and culture which at a given moment can fuse harmoniously human duality vis-à-vis the complexity of a particular moment in history. Creativity must deal with the reality that nothing in the human world is static.

In reference to the dynamics of reality, Jung speaks of the archetypes, the psychic dominants of the human soul, as also cosmic, as belonging to a world soul. Life is larger than humanity. Therefore, creativity in the larger sense of participation in the ongoing creation must remain always in the light of the stars, that is, close to the currents and inspirations of the larger archetypal energies, those forces which are beyond human conception, yet, enter abruptly into the human world and must be reckoned with. In the end, like Job who must recognize and reckon with powers greater than he; an individual for all one's fecundity and power, must return with humility unto oneself and in this way comes to truly know oneself. Self knowledge in the end comes from the recognition of one's limitations, failures, and insignificance in the face of powers greater than oneself. However, like Job, an individual's humble acceptance of power, responsibility, and self knowledge, brings with it, without the asking, fruitfulness, abundance, and blessedness.

The symbolism of the sixth day suggests that the fullness of the creative life can be realized only when an individual assumes with humility and grace one's rightful power in the universe, and that only through the acceptance of this awesome responsibility, and all the difficulties, triumphs, and failures that go with it, can an individual truly know onesellf. On the sixth day, "God saw that it was very good"—not only good, but very good. Moral integrity and purpose is confirmed; blessedness and rest are now called for.

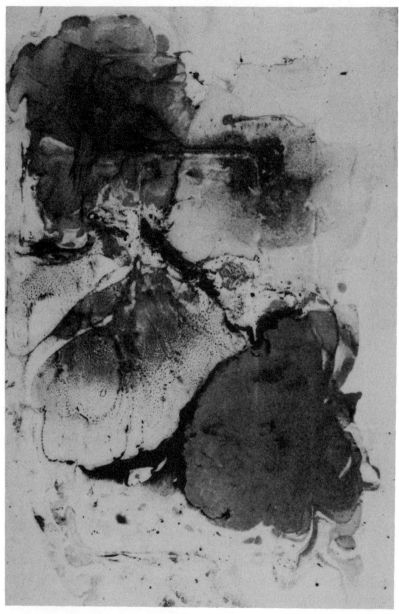

The heavens and the earth were
finished and all the host of them

Lorraine Fink

THE SEVENTH DAY

> Thus the heavens and the earth were fin-
> ished, and all the host of them. And on the
> seventh day God finished his work which he
> had done, and he rested on the seventh day
> from all his work which he had done. So God
> blessed the seventh day and hallowed it,
> because on it God rested from all his work
> which he had done in creation.
> Genesis 2:1-3

On the seventh day the heavens and the earth are finished, and all the host of them. If heaven symbolizes an ideal whose lights guide one's creativity, one's world, then the plural, "heavens" and "all the hosts of them" suggest many creative projects and creative experiences for a lifetime. When one has done and lived them all—only then can one rest. No rest until the end.

The seventh day is blessed and hallowed. One does not work on this day. Rest means inactivity, a return to the oneness, to the unity of one's being to be blessed and hallowed. This is another dimension of reality. On the sixth day when an individaul has reckoned with the fullness of productivity and power, that person comes at last to finality. Until an individual comes full circle to the end of one's work, and projection of oneself, the individual cannot truly arrive at self knowledge. It is on the sixth day that God makes human beings in His own image; the imagery suggests that on the sixth day true self knowledge is possible. Once this happens, a person has transcended oneself, the dynamic creativity that one was. On the seventh day, the individual has moved beyond one's former dynamics to another dimension of reality to be blessed and hallowed. Blessedness is much more than completion. It is the fullness of life that has now moved beyond life as we know it, for the life has fulfilled its purpose and no longer goes on in this world. One might call such an individual a saint, but the saint is no longer in time. In the world of time, saints are hallowed, remembered, and revered. A creative life, a creative work, leaves a mark in the world. It has made a contribution to the ongoing creation which belongs to the world of time. But the saint, that individual who has fulfilled one's purpose and made a contribution to life, has gone to rest.

Rest ultimately means death. Death is welcomed. As Jung says, only those who fear life, fear death. A foolish disregard for death belongs to those who do not respect life. But for those who have truly valued life and have lived it to the full, death is a crowning glory. To have lived one's life to the full guided by the lights of heaven, to have finished one's "heaven and the earth and all the hosts of them" is the culmination of a life, whose meaning the individual can discover finally when one is ultimately separated from life in the world.

"To be made in the image of God" suggests coming full circle to know oneself. When a person finally succeeds in doing this, one can rest and return unto oneself. When all of the projections of oneself and all of one's possibilities in life have been realized, an individual can rest in death. Only the unlived life, not the fullness of life, causes unrest and fear of death. One's sins committed in living too much can be repented and forgiven, but one's lost opportunities, one's failures to live, can never be regained. Hence the age-old belief in multiple lifetimes. Life can run out and death can come without rest. Rest belongs only to those who have truly lived. Only then can a life be blessed and hallowed.

COMMENTARY

The seventh day completes the cycle of birth and death in the creative life, a life lived in the human world of time. But the creative principle alone is not the whole of a human life. In Jung's terminology, the creative spirit is the dynamic aspect of the higher Self, which is the principle of unity, the central archetype in the human personality. In the myth, God has been interpreted as the higher self in human beings, as that organizing driving force in a human life that directs the energies and impells one forward to life and consciousness in higher and more differentiated forms. Lesser archetypes (less in the sense that no one of them alone is central to the personality) are symbolized by the sun, moon, stars, and other images in the myth. They are included in their general aspects, but their full delineation in the unfolding development of the human psyche is not given in the imagery of this myth. For example, the masculine and feminine dominants are portrayed in their primordial beginnings in consciousness as cosmic principles and as human necessities for nurture and order, but their dynamic interaction is not depicted in this myth. However, in Jung's terminology, one could say that developing consciousness of these other energies is dependent upon an initial separation of ego consciousness from unconsciousness. This dawning awareness is the beginning of adult life, and, from the Jungian perspective, the beginning of the path of individuation.

The seven days of creation, therefore, have been interpreted as a map for this path, a map which is seminal to consciousness at the beginning of the journey. Throughout the interpretation, attention as been given the role of the will, that imperative in the myth which calls for each new stage of development. Adult creative life is not forced on human beings. One might say that the essence of being human is to have the option to refuse life and consciousness in more highly evolved forms. On the other hand, the mystery of why all forms of human life do not evolve has been left open. Will, with its consequences, belongs only to those who recognize it. Likewise, the value of human creativity and consciousness vis-à-vis nature and unconsciousness cannot be measured solely by human standards. As Jung indicates, the path of individuation is a vocation. I add, like faith it is both a gift and an act of the will. The irrational facts of experience are given, but the conscious, moral integration of these facts is a choice. While the final meaning of life awaits discovery at the moment of death, its ultimate critique is beyond both life and death.

CHAPTER 11

All references to C. G. Jung's works, unless otherwise indicated, are taken from the *Collected Works* (C. W.) second edition, 20 vols., Princeton University Press.

1. *The Oxford Annotated Bible* (New York: Oxford University Press, 1962).

2. "Psychology and Literature" (1950), C. W. 15:101-102 (157).

3. "The Structure of the Unconscious" (1947), C. W. 7:293-294 (4-499).

4. *Timaeus* 86b-87d, *The Collected Dialogues of Plato Including the Letters,* edited by Edith Hamilton and Huntington Cairnes; Bollingen Series LXXI (New York: Pantheon Books, 1966), pp. 1206-1207.

5. Susanne K. Langer, *Feeling and Form* (New York, 1953).

6. *The Republic* 517b-c, *The Collected Dialogues of Plato,* pp. 749-750.

7. "The Structure of the Psyche" (1931), C. W. 8:152 (325).

8. Edward G. Ballard, *Art and Analysis: An Essay Toward a Theory in Aesthetics* (The Hague: Martinus Nijhoff, 1971), p. 193.

CONCLUSION

This work represents an effort to articulate philosophical conceptions found in Jung's writings, particularly those ideas which relate to contemporary questions in philosophy. Jung has a theory of knowledge which is related to a more comprehensive view of the human psyche and an implied metaphysics which integrates the physical and psychic realms. He has a theory of humanity which combines not only an awareness of evil and a positive faith, but also a creative involvement in the human/cosmic process. Jung has a psychology which lends itself to a theory of art and aesthetics, which transcends purely subjective criteria to participate in a broad theory of value related to ancient and universal modes. Within his psychology, Jung offers the basis of a theory of education which goes beyond the pragmatic needs of any particular social climate or moment of history and points to a more comprehsensive view of the whole person.

In the field of epistemology, Jung's theory of knowledge in part is related to his conception of the structure of the human mind and in part to outer empirical data. Jung cannot be labeled simply as an empiricist versus an idealist, or a rationalist versus a mystic. In a sense, he is all of these, for his method which derives from a fourfold conception of the human psyche, is not limited to any single epistemological perspective. Furthermore, his view of the primordial state of the human psyche, as one of tension needing the continual resolution of opposing energies, lends itself to a dynamic theory which at once grounds all systems of thought and remains open to the new.

Jung called himself an empiricist, but he has been criticized by those to whom the word "empirical" means conformity to strict canons of verifiability. Jung has been criticized for his undefined methods of gathering and classifying data, and hence the claim is made that he never succeeded in finding an established science to which he might refer as a paradigm of his own methods.[1]

In answering this criticism, one must first take into consideration Jung's conception of his method of psychotherapy. While sensitive to the methods of other psychologists, Jung's early association experiments attest to his view that psychoanalysis is essentially a way of investigating unconscious associations which cannot be got at by exploring the conscious mind. He saw psychoanalysis as a method (or perhaps a group of methods) which makes possible the analytical reduction of psychic contents to their simplest expression in order to discover the line of least resistance in the development of a harmonious personality. He held that the main principle of psychoanalytic technique is to analyze the psychic contents that present themselves at a given moment and that any interference on the part of the analyst with the object of forcing the analysis to follow a systematic course was a gross mistake. He believed that so-called chance is the law and order of psychoanalysis.[2] Thus, he viewed his method as purely empirical and as totally lacking any final theoretical framework; it was simply the quickest way to find facts of importance for psychology. However, he acknowledged that the history of psychology shows other more tedious and complicated ways of also attaining these facts.[3]

For Jung, psychotherapy was a kind of dialectical process, a dialogue or discussion between two persons. He compared his method to the dialectic of the ancient philosophers, which was orginally the art of conversation, a process creating new syntheses. In this situation, a person can be seen as a psychic system, which, when it affects another person, enters into reciprocal reaction with another psychic system.[4] Thus, one can see that fundamentally Jung's method of psychotherapy was also philosophical in the classic sense, a dialectic whose dynamics brought to consiousness not only a more complete understanding of the problem involved, but also the emergence of a new insight.

Jung believed that since the psyche is infinitely complicated, many antinomies are required to describe its nature satisfactorily. Furthermore, contradictions show that only relatively valid statements can be made and that a statement is valid only in so far as it indicates what kind of psychic system is being investigated. Since the individuality of the psychic system is infinitely variable, an infinite variety of relatively valid statements must follow. However, individuality is not absolute in its particularity. One individual is not totally different from every other individual, otherwise psychology would be impossible as a science. It would consist in an insoluble chaos of subjective opinions. Individuality, therefore, is only relative, the complement of human conformity or likeness.

Jung concluded that to treat another individual psychologically at all, one must for better or worse give up all pretensions to superior knowledge, all authority and desire to influence. One must adopt a dialectical procedure consisting of a comparison of mutual findings. The other person must be given a chance to play one's hand to the full unhampered by the therapist's assumptions. In this way, Jung said, the patient's psychic system is geared to Jung's and acts upon it. Jung's reaction was the only thing with which he as an individual could legitimately confront his patient. He insisted that a doctor allow the patient to find the patient's own philosophical, social, and political bent because the precondition for responsible action is that a person should know oneself and one's peculiarities and have the courage to stand by them. Only when an individual lives in this way is one responsible and capable of action.

One can see that for Jung method was of secondary importance. He believed the more deeply we penetrate the nature of the psyche the more the conviction grows that the diversity, the multi-dimensionality of human nature requires the greatest variety of standpoints and methods in order to satisfy the variety of psychic dispositions.[5] From his point of view, the greatest healing factor in psychotherapy is the doctor's personality, which is something not given at the start; instead, it represents the doctor's performance at its highest and not a doctrinaire blueprint. He quoted an ancient adept as saying: "If the wrong man uses the right means, the right means work in the wrong way."[6] This Chinese saying stands in sharp contrast to the belief in the "right" method irrespective of the person who applies it. For Jung everything depends on the person and little or nothing on the method, for method is merely the path, the direction taken by a person. The way one acts is the true expression of one's nature. Jung believed that if a method is not this, it is nothing more than an affectation, something artificially added on, rootless and sapless. serving only the illegitimate goal of self-satisfaction. It becomes a means of fooling oneself, of evading what may perhaps be the implacable law of one's being. This emphasis on the individual and on the variety and spontaneity of methods in the dialectical encounter between doctor and patient characterizes the essentially creative process which Jung viewed as psychoanalysis.

The methodology of all of Jung's work dealing with the unconscious was likewise a creative process and in this sense was beyond the verification procedures required of a theory limited exclusively to the natural sciences. Jung's life and work flow together in a continuous creative effort, which can be described only in part by a conscious intention and scrutiny. On the contrary, this effort was just as much subject to irrational inspirations and meanderings of the spirit. For example, Jung's entire sojourn in the images of his own unconscious, and later in the symbology of Gnosticism and alchemy, was prompted by an inspiration, a creative urge to search for hidden truths in unknown territory and in half-forgotten symbolic systems. His motivation was sparked by creative insight and not by rational decision alone. Jung used the empirical method to the degree that he observed phenomena and collated data in line with "hypotheses"— creative hunches which came to him through dreams and reflective insight. The inspirations came first and the methods of inquiry followed—not the other way around.

The same can be said for Jung's hermeneutic method linked to his theory of archetypes. Jung began with the image presented to him through his dreams, outer events, his patients' images, and other unexpected sources; from the image itself in its context he searched for analogues. Hence, no precise dictionary of symbols can exist in the Jungian method,[7] for the referents of the image along with meaning possibilities vary from one context to the next. For Jung every image is unique in its time-space continuum. Jung's theory of the archetypes, however, in no way foreshadows this uniqueness. Instead, it can be regarded as the guide for the search. Archetypes point to a "family of meanings," to use Wittengenstein's terminology as applied to an image; an image represents one example of a generic category of meanings. An image participates in this category and shares its associations to the degree that at the same time it preserves its uniqueness and hence its special meaning in the time-space continuum. The verification of the special meaning discovered in this way lies in what Jung calls its "intense value for life." He says that if the fantasy (or image) is understood in this way hermeneutically as an authentic symbol, it then acts as a signpost, providing the clues one needs in order to carry on one's life in harmony with oneself. This point of view, however, has worth only to those who believe that human beings should take charge of their lives rather than live simply by principles proven rationally to be right.[8]

The above principle will be the point of departure for those contemporary philosophers who espouse only a theory of "public" truth, that is, the truth of the collective limited by the methodology of the physical and social sciences. Jung would balance the collective view with the intuitive insight offered by the inner image and the inner voice. Only this balance permits the whole person to move with certainty along one's unique life lines.

Jung's optimism regarding personal truth is related to his theory of reality in which human beings participate. For Jung, the individual is not a bystander doomed to observe a fated world or a meaningless process. A person is an active participant in the cosmic drama and has the role of contributing positively or negatively to the ongoing creation. Through consciousness and moral action, one can creatively contribute to the future in a fruitful way. However, Jung warns that this optimistic hope rests upon one's willingess to confront one's negative side—the individual's shadow. The cure for the ills of the world, Jung believed, lies not in collective politics and power, nor in well-meaning humanitarian motives and actions, but in individual realization and confrontation with the reality of both creative and destructive forces in the human psyche remaining largely below the surface of consciousness. In this way, Jung held that the hope of the world rests upon the development of human consciousness and morality. His theory of humanity differs markedly from that of many psychologists and sociologists today who see human beings only in terms of positive, constructive forces within, while relegating all problems of evil in the individual and society to external conditions and causes. For Jung, as for the Taoists, the inner and outer worlds reflect each other. Evil and destruction exist in the world because evil and destruction exist in human beings which they willingly or unwillingly fail to recognize. For Jung, no amount of social action and guarantee of social security in a material sense can remove human beings from their primordial condition which is a tension between opposite forces in their very nature. Jung once wrote that as social security increases, psychic security decreases. When one identifies exclusively with positive forces, the destructive ones creep up from behind. The only way to deal effectively with this primordial situation, according to Jung, is to become sensitive in true perspective to the shadow side of oneself and then do something about it.

Just as Jung's theory of reality including humanity integrates positive and negative forces, as well as human participation in the cosmic drama, so does his theory of art. The great masterpieces of civilization mirror the soul of humanity engaged in the world. Great art lays hold of the grand archetypal themes of an age through the uniqueness of a single perspective—that of the individual artist. Jung's theory of the archetypes provides a clue to a more profound understanding of the formal structures of the arts, while his insistence on human transcendence is the essential key to sensing art's greatness.

Likewise, Jung's view of education incorporates a more spiritual attitude, especially as applied to education for the second half of life. Jung's fourfold model of the human psyche should provide theorists with a larger and more complex understanding of human needs and possibilities of development. What is of significance for the first half of life when the development of the ego requires expansion in the world is of less importance in the second half when the need for a more profound understanding of life's purpose is felt.

Jung's insistence on the special needs for education in the more mature years, for life's enrichment as well as for preparation for death, places educational goals as a whole in an entirely different light. Education of the whole person demands a comprehensive view which is neglected by theorists who attend primarily to pragmatic goals. We need to educate human feelings and emotions, imagination and spiritual powers, as well as to develop physical and cognitive skills. An individual needs to be educated to live with refinement and sensitivity, with moral consciousness and purpose, as well as to earn a living. But most of all, in Jung's view, education must allow the individual to develop, for the creative spirit lies not in the collective mass, but in the individual where it can take root and flower.

Emphasis on the importance of individual growth in consciousness is a corollary to Jung's myth of meaning. The goal of human existence and of reality as a whole for Jung is consciousness. All of nature depends on humanity for consciousness. Beyond consciousness as the highest aim of nature is meaning. The goal of life, then, is the discovery of meaning—the meaning of one's existence, which contributes in some small part to the total collective consciousness. For Jung, meaning is the ultimte value, and meaning is in essence individual. Jung said that as the body needs food—not just any kind of food but only that which suits it—the psyche needs to know the meaning of its existence—not just any meaning, but the meaning of those images and ideas which reflect its nature and which originate in the unconscious. The unconscious supplies the archetypal form, which in itself is empty and irrepresentable. Consciousness immediately fills it with related or similar representational material so that it can be perceived.[9]

Jung said we do not know how far the process of coming to consciousness can extend or where it will lead. Since it is a new element in the story of creation with no parallels one can look to, we cannot know what potentialities are inherent in it. However, in our mythic statements we frame a view of the world which adequately explains the meaning of human existence in the cosmos, a view which springs from our psychic wholeness, from the cooperation between conscious and unconscious. Meaninglessness, on the other hand, inhibits the fullness of life and is therefore equivalent to illness, whereas meaning makes almost everything endurable.[10]

Myth which renders meaning cannot be made out of science or replaced by science because myth cannot be invented. For Jung, myth is the revelation of a divine life in humanity. It confronts human beings spontaneously and places obligations upon them but is not affected by the arbitrary operations of the will. As the child of inspiration, myth cannot be explained or reduced to anything else. The chief feeling about divine inspiration is that it comes from elsewhere.

However, everything through which this "other will" is expressed proceeds from human beings—their thinking, words, images, and even their limitations. Hence, Jung says, a person has the tendency to refer everything to oneself when one begins to think in clumsy psychological terms and decides that everything proceeds out of one's intentions and out of oneself. Whereas in reality myth happens, and only through great effort does an individual succed in recognizing that one is confronting instinctive foundations given from the beginning. These beginnings are the constant substratum of one's existence and consciousness and are as much molded by them as by the physical world. Awareness of these foundations gives an individual insight into myths and leads one to the discovery of meaning in life.

Myths give an approximate description of an unconscious core of meaning which can never be made fully conscious. This core, or archetype, is only interpreted, and every interpretation that comes anywhere near the hidden sense, right from the beginning lays claim not only to absolute truth and validity, but also to instant reverence and religious devotion. For Jung, the core of myth, the archetypes, are living psychic forces that demand to be taken seriously and have a strange way of making sure of their effect. They cannot be denied or neutralized. Consequently, at every new stage in the development of consciousness humanity is confronted with the task of finding a new interpretation of myth appropriate to the new stage in order to connect the life in the past that still exists with the life of the present which threatens to slip away from it.[11] Without this link-up, Jung said, a rootless consciousness comes into being no longer oriented to the past, a consciousness which succumbs helplessly to all manner of suggestions and in practice is susceptible to psychic epidemics. Hence human beings must dream the myth onwards and give it a modern dress, for the archetype is an element of psychic structure and thus a vital and necessary component in psychic economy. It represents or personifies instinctive data of the primitive psyche, the invisible roots of consciousness for which no rational substitute exists.

On the other hand, Jung warns, the differentiated consciousness of the civilized person through the dynamics of one's will has been granted an effective instrument for the practical realization of its aims. Yet the more an individual trains the will, all the more danger occurs of getting lost in one-sidedness and deviating further from the laws and roots of one's being.[12] Differentiated consciousness is in continual danger of being uprooted. Progress enforced by will is always convulsive; the progressive ideal is always more abstract, more unnatural, and less "moral" for it demands disloyalty to tradition. But the older view realizes that true progress is possible through consciousness of opposites and repetition of the age-old rituals on a higher plane. Viable progress comes from the cooperation of a differentiated consciousness with the age-old roots of its being in the primitive psyche through the preservation and updated viability of ancient myths. Only in this way can a person stay in touch with primordial beginnings and at the same time discover the unfolding meaning of one's indiviudal life. From this point of view, Jung's "myth of meaning" is the underlying metaphor of his entire philosophy.

After this overview of Jung's basic philosophical ideas and presentation of his concept of method and view of myth, one may ask, what are the other criticisms of Jung? Jung himself would answer that his theories did not go far enough. In one lifetime, Jung opened many doors, including some not mentioned in this work, and he regretted that he could not develop his insights further. For example, Jung's theory of synchronicity with its background as the archetype of number was, he felt, insufficiently developed. Also, his view of the human psyche was, he believed, only a beginning. He said that we know almost nothing about the human psyche, but the need for knowledge is imperative, since we hold the power of destruction in our hands.

Furthermore, some hold that Jung's understanding of the feminine psyche is limited, since Jung viewed eros or relatedness as the essentially feminine mode, whereas the feminine archetypes are many and varied and each in time, in turn, or in an age may dominate the feminine ego.[13] Jung's theory of the feminine as woman herself, more so than a man's anima, needs further development, a challenge which some of his followers have assumed.

The criticism is also made that Jung was more of a mystic than a scientist (or a philosopher). To those who hold that Jung was essentially a mystic, I offer this answer (in addition to chapter 10). A mystic experiences union with the absolute and annihilates one's existence in the presence of the absolute. Jung did not do this. Up until his last dream and his final moment he was firmly his own person, his individual self. A mystic is lost in love—love of God or the absolute or nature. The mystical union is the union of oneself with the Other; "I live not I but Thou livest in me." Jung, however, lived his own life. Philemon, the archetypal wise old man, lived in him as his number two personality, but Jung lived consciously in his contemporary life. Jung said he knew God; he did not identify his existence with God. He lived in the world with his wife, family, close friends, colleagues, and patients, and with nature. He was not lost in the love of the absolute.

Furthermore, Jung saw his own existence as significant, as having meaning. At the end of his life, his dreams told him he had done his work well. A mystic, on the contrary, sees all that one does as worthless in the face of the Divine. The mystic's existence is of little importance.

All of these facts confirm the thesis that Jung was more of a philosopher than a mystic. A philosopher looks for meaning; a mystic seeks union. Jung's myth was a myth of meaning, not a myth of love and union.

For Jung, love was explained as archetypal projection and transference, and as leading to the wholeness of the individual personality. In this context, love is a means, not an end in itself, a means to the highest value—the discovery of the meaning of one's life.

In this regard, Jung is more Greek than Christian. The Greek dramatists teach that wisdom (meaning) comes through suffering the tragedies of life, while the Greek philosophers saw wisdom as the culmination of intellectual and moral virtue and hence as the highest value.

Christianity teaches that God is love. The highest value is love and dedication of one's life and purpose to the spread of love (the two commandments of Christianity). Meaning is secondary, or better, only comes through love. Jung saw the Christianity of his father and of his environment as out of touch with the needs of the people and as the manifestation of an outdated theology. Even though he embraced Christianity as his cultural heritage and had great respect for the older forms of Christian ritual and belief which incorporated the feminine principle, Jung was not a Christian mystic, nor was Christian love his highest value.

Jung was a healer of human beings, but what led him into this profession was not primarily a philanthropic desire to help humanity. In his autobiography, he recounts his prime motivation as his curiosity about the human psyche and the very practical necessity to choose a profession in conjunction with his interest. In all of his healing, he was searching for truth as much as helping his patients.

However, we cannot say that in emphasizing meaning Jung downgraded love. In his work on alchemy, Jung speaks of love as the union of opposites. The royal marriage is a symbol for the supreme and ultimate union representing the magic-by-analogy which brings the alchemical work to its final consummation and binds the opposites by love, for "love is stronger than death."[14] The metaphysical ideal founded on love was the opposite of the pagan ideal of worldly power, for "where force rules, there is no love, and where love reigns force does not count"—an age-old truth which found its expression in Christianity.

Jung refers to Jesus as obeying the inner call of his vocation and voluntarily exposing himself to the assaults of the imperialistic madness that in his time filled everyone, conqueror and conquered alike. Far from suppressing or allowing himself to be suppressed by this psychic onslaught, Jesus let it act on him consciously and assimilated it. Thus, world conquering Caesarism was transformed into spiritual worship and the Roman Empire into the universal kingdom of God that was not of this world. Wordly power was transformed into spiritual love.[15] However, of his own time, Jung wrote. "....the greater part of Europe has succumbed to neo-paganism and anti-Christianity, and has set up a religious ideal of worldly power in opposition to the metaphysical ideal founded on love."[16]

Power is of this world, whereas love operates through an unworldly principle. In the truly Christian perspective, the intangible force of love takes precedence over the worldly forces that can be seen. From the viewpoint of Jung's metaphysics, the transcendent function, or love as the union of opposites, is the ultimate life principle which goes beyond nature and the powers of the visible world. The transcendent dimension of human life operates at an archetypal level more powerful than all of the other archetypes combined, for it is intimately linked to the central archetype of the Self, the giver of all inner and outer experience. Hence, the call of the Self, manifested by vocation, binds the individual with love and transforms one into the doer of deeds imposed from on high. This love Jung extolls, not the romantic and sentimental love more familiar to the modern age. Jung's myth of meaning includes the Christian myth of love in the highest sense, for by way of understanding, the individual can interpret one's call to the active duty of life which binds one through love, and by reflection can comprehend from a later vantage point its ultimate significance and value for oneself and for humanity.

Consequently, Jung's myth of meaning, through an incorporation of the love which binds the individual to one's vocation, has a message for those well-intentioned people who want to do good in the world. Bombarded by advances in technology, overwhelmed by powers of destruction, and with all of their values put into question vis-à-vis conflicting ideologies, good people ask if their lives have any significance. Jung has an answer in his theory of individuation wherein every single increment of consciousness contributes to collective consciousness. Since collectively all human beings are one, in a sense, through a state of participation mystique, what anyone knows or does affects everyone else, even if only imperceptibly. From this perspective, one's enlightenment and fidelity to life's meaning and goal, contribute to the enlightenment of all and to the accumulation of positive energy in the environment.

From the Jungian standpoint, good people would do better to turn first to the development of their consciousness with a realization of their darker side before directing their efforts to humanitarian goals. In this way, their enlightened love would result in a more authentic effort toward world peace and well being.

If one can understand Jung's myth of meaning as incorporating love in the highest sense and if one can appreciate Jung's method of inquiry as an essentially creative enterprise, might one still disagree with Jung's synthesis? Yes, one might disagree with him from the outset by not accepting his premises regarding the following: the spiritual dimension of human beings, the universe as psychophysical, the problem of evil and destruction as related to human unconsciousness, the theory of the unconscious as personal and collective, language and symbolic forms as prior to rational intentions, the relevance of history and culture to an understanding of contemporary life, and other possible views which are starting points in his system of thought. In these instances, one's fundamental intuitions about humanity and reality would be different from Jung's, and consequently Jung would have little to offer. As I stated in the introduction of this book, philosophical presuppositions are rooted in psychological orientations to reality. I hope this work has shed some light on the orientation which is the basis of Jung's myth and will thereby help the critical reader to clarify one's possible points of departure.

On the other hand, one may accept some or all of Jung's premises but feel that Jung is inconsistent in his theories, which may especially be the case if one reads only some of his works without studying Jung's thought as a whole. In his intellectual evolution, Jung continued to revise his ideas and rewrote many of his papers as his intuitions were refined and his thoughts matured. Jung was critical of himself, and his ideas deepened and developed in the course of his life and work. Therefore, the ideas which Jung expressed in later life may best reflect his final synthesis.

In conclusion, the aim of this work when faced with Jung's tremendous contribution to culture has been primarily expository with the hope that more intellectuals will take the time to study— and appreciate—Jung as a philosopher of the first rank. I believe future generations will see C.G. Jung as one of the giants of the twentieth century who sought to restore the two dimensions of human thinking (rational and non rational) to their essential unity in creative intellectual life. Without this unity, speculative philosophy cannot progress.

204

CONCLUSION

All references to C. G. Jung's works, unless otherwise indicated, are taken from the *Collected Works* (C. W.) second edition, 20 vols., Princeton University Press.

1. James W. Heisig, *Imago Dei: A Study of C. G. Jung's Psychology of Religion* (Lewisburg, Pa.: Bucknell University Press; London: Associated University Press, 1979) p. 140.

2. "Some Crucial Points in Psychoanalysis" (1916), C. W., 4:272 (625).

3. "On the Criticism of Psychoanalysis" (1910), C. W., 4:75 (195).

4. "Principles of Practical Psychotherapy" (1935), C. W., 16:3 (1).

5. *Ibid.* 9 (11).

6. "Commentary on 'The Secret of the Golden Flower' " (1938), C. W., 13:7 (4).

7. *C. G. Jung Letters,* ed. G. Adler and A. Jaffe, trans. R. F. C. Bollingen Series XCV:2 (Princeton: Princeton University Press), vol. 2, p. 123.

8. "The Structure of the Unconscious" (1916), C. W., 7:291 (493).

9. "The Philosophical Tree" (1954), C. W. 13:346 (476).

10. C. G. Jung, *Memories, Dreams, Reflections,* recorded and edited by Aniela Jaffe, translated from the German by Richard and Clara Winston (New York: Vintage Books, 1963), p. 340.

11. "The Psychology of the Child Archetype" (1963), C. W., 9-1: 157 (267).

12. *Ibid.* 162-163 (276).

13. Jean Shinoda Bolen, *Goddesses in Every Woman* (New York: Harper and Row, 1984).

14. "The Psychology of the Transference" (1946), C. W., 16:198 (398).

15. "The Development of Personality" (1934), C. W., 17: 180 (309).

16. "The Psychology of the Transference" *op. cit.,* 196 (397).

BIBLIOGRAPHY

A.   WORKS BY C. G. JUNG

I—THE COLLECTED WORKS

The publication of the first complete edition, in English of the works of C. G. Jung was undertaken by Routledge and Kegan Paul Ltd., in England and by Bollingen Foundation in the United States. The American edition is number XX in Bollingen Series, which since 1967 has been published by Princeton University Press. The edition contains revised versions of works previously published, such as *Psychology of the Unconscious,* which is now entitled *Symbols of Transformation;* works originally written in English, such as *Psychology and Religion;* works not previously translated, such as *Aion;* and, in general, new translations of virtually all of Professor Jung's writings. Prior to his death, in 1961, the author supervised the textual revision, which in some cases is extensive. Sir Herbert Read (d. 1968), Dr. Michael Fordham, and Dr. Gerhard Adler compose the Editorial Committee; the translator is R.F.C. Hull (except for Volume 2) and William McGuire is executive director.

Vol. 1.   PSYCHIATRIC STUDIES (1957, 1970)
   On the Psychology and Pathology of So-Called Occult Phenomena (1902)
   On Hysterical Misreading (1904)
   Cryptomnesia (1905)
   On Manic Mood Disorder (1903)
   A Case of Hysterical Stupor in a Prisoner in Detention (1902)
   On Simulated Insanity (1903)
   A Medical Opinion on a Case of Simulated Insanity (1904)
   A Third and Final Opinion on Two Contradictory Psychiatric Diagnoses (1906)
   On the Psychological Diagnosis of Facts (1905)

206

Vol. 2. EXPERIMENTAL RESEARCHES (1973)
Translated by Leopold Stein in collaboration with Diana Riviere
Studies in Word Association (1904-7, 1910)
The Associations of Normal Subjects (by Jung and F. Riklin)
An Analysis of the Associations of an Epileptic
The Reaction-Time Ratio in the Association Experiment
Experimental Observations on the Faculty of Memory
Psychoanalysis and Association Experiments
The Psychological Diagnosis of Evidence
Association, Dream, and Hysterical Symptom
The Psychopathological Significance of the Association Experiment
Disturbances in Reproduction in the Association Experiment
The Association Method
The Family Constellation

Psychophysical Researches (1907-8)
On the Psychophysical Relations of the Association Experiment
Psychophysical Investigations with the Galvanometer and Pneumograph in Normal and Insane Individuals (by F. Peterson and Jung)
Further Investigations on the Galvanic Phenomenon and Respiration in Normal and Insane Individuals (by C. Ricksher and Jung)
Appendix: Statistical Details of Enlistment (1906); New Aspects of Criminal Psychology (1908); The Psychological Methods of Investigation Used in the Psychiatric Clinic of the University of Zurich (1910); On the Doctrine of Complexes ([1911], 1913); On the Psychological Diagnosis of Evidence (1937)

Vol. 3. THE PSYCHOGENESIS OF MENTAL DISEASE (1960)
The Psychology of Dementia Praecox (1907)
The Content of the Psychoses (1908/1914)
On Psychological Understanding (1914)
A Criticism of Bleuler's Theory of Schizophrenic Nega-

On the Importance of the Unconscious in Psycho-
pathology (1914)
On the Problem of Psychogenesis in Mental Disease
(1919)
Mental Disease and the Psyche (1928)
On the Psychogenesis of Schizophrenia (1939)
Recent Thoughts on Schizophrenia (1957)
Schizophrenia (1958)

Vol. 4.   FREUD AND PSYCHOANALYSIS (1961)
Freud's Theory of Hysteria: A Reply to Aschaffenburg
(1906)
The Freudian Theory of Hysteria (1908)
The Analysis of Dreams (1909)
A Contribution to the Psychology of Rumor (1910-11)
On the Significance of Number Dreams (1910-11)
Morton Prince, "The Mechanism and Interpretation of
Dreams": A Critical Review (1911)
On the Criticism of Psychoanalysis (1910)
Concerning Psychoanalysis (1912)
The Theory of Psychoanalysis (1913)
General Aspects of Psychoanalysis (1913)
Psychoanalysis and Neurosis (1916)
Some Crucial Points in Psychoanalysis: A Correspon-
dence between Dr. Jung and Dr. Loÿ (1914)
Prefaces to "Collected Papers on Analytical Psychology"
(1916-1917)
The Significance of the Father in the Destiny of the
Individual (1909/1949)
Introduction to Kranefeldt's "Secret Ways of the Mind"
(1930)
Freud and Jung: Contrasts (1929)

Vol. 5.   SYMBOLS OF TRANSFORMATION
(1911-12/1952, 1956, 1967)
PART I
Introduction
Two Kinds of Thinking
The Miller Fantasies: Anamnesis

The Hymn of Creation
The Song of the Moth

PART II
Introduction
The Concept of Libido
The Transformation of Libido
The Origin of the Hero
Symbols of the Mother and of Rebirth
The Battle for Deliverance from the Mother
The Dual Mother
The Sacrifice
Epilogue
Appendix: The Miller Fantasies

Vol. 6.   PSYCHOLOGICAL TYPES (1921, 1971)
Introduction
The Problem of Types in the History of Classical and
    Medieval Thought
Schiller's Ideas on the Type Problem
The Apollinian and the Dionysian
The Type Problem in Human Character
The Type Problem in Poetry
The Type Problem in Psychopathology
The Type Problem in Aesthetics
The Type Problem in Modern Philosophy
The Type Problem in Biography
General Description of the Types
Definitions
Epilogue
Four Papers on Psychological Typology (1913, 1925,
    1931, 1936)

Vol. 7.   TWO ESSAYS ON ANALYTICAL PSYCHOLOGY
    (1953, 1966)
On the Psychology of the Unconscious (1917/1926/1943)
The Relations between the Ego and the Unconscious
    (1928)
Appendix: New Paths in Psychology (1912); The Struc-
    ture of the Unconscious (1916) (new versions, with
    variants, 1966)

Vol. 8.   THE STRUCTURE AND DYNAMICS OF THE
          PSYCHE (1960, 1969)
          On Psychic Energy (1928)
          The Transcendent Function ([1916]/1957)
          A Review of the Complex Theory (1934)
          The Significance of Constitution and Heredity in Psy-
          chology (1929)
          Psychological Factors Determining Human Behavior
          (1937)
          Instinct and the Unconscious (1919)
          The Structure of the Psyche (1927/1931)
          On the Nature of the Psyche (1947/1954)
          General Aspects of Dream Psychology (1916/1948)
          On the Nature of Dreams (1945/1948)
          The Psychological Foundations of Belief in Spirits
          (1920/1948)
          Spirit and Life (1926)
          Basic Postulates of Analytical Psychology (1931)
          Analytical Psychology and *Weltanschauung* (1928/1931)
          The Real and the Surreal (1933)
          The Soul and Death (1934)
          Synchronicity: An Acausal Connecting Principle (1952)
          Appendix: On Synchronicity (1951)

Vol. 9.   PART I. THE ARCHETYPES AND THE COLLEC-
          TIVE UNCONSCIOUS (1959, 1968)
          Archetypes of the Collective Unconscious (1934/1954)
          The Concept of the Collective Unconscious (1936)
          Concerning the Archetypes, with Special Reference to
          the Anima Concept (1946/1954)
          Psychological Aspects of the Mother Archetype
          (1938/1954)
          Concerning Rebirth (1940/1950)
          The Psychology of the Child Archetype (1940)
          The Psychological Aspects of the Kore (1941)
          The Phenomenology of the Spirit in Fairytales
          (1945/1948)
          On the Psychology of the Trickster-Figure (1954)
          Conscious, Unconscious, and Individuation (1939)
          A Study in the Process of Individuation (1934/1950)

210

Concerning Mandala Symbolism (1950)
Appendix: Mandalas (1955)

Vol. 9.   PART II. AION (1951, 1959, 1968)
RESEARCHES INTO THE PHENOMENOLOGY OF THE SELF
The Ego
The Shadow
The Syzygy: Anima and Animus
The Self
Christ, a Symbol of the Self
The Sign of the Fishes
The Prophecies of Nostradamus
The Historical Significance of the Fish
The Ambivalence of the Fish Symbol
The Fish in Alchemy
The Alchemical Interpretation of the Fish
Background to the Psychology of Christian Alchemical
   Symbolism
Gnostic Symbols of the Self
The Structure and Dynamics of the Self
Conclusion

Vol. 10. CIVILIZATION IN TRANSITION (1964, 1970)
The Role of the Unconcious (1918)
Mind and Earth (1927/1931)
Archaic Man (1931)
The Spiritual Problem of Modern Man (1928/1931)
The Love Problem of a Student (1928)
Women in Europe (1927)
The Meaning of Psychology for Modern Man (1933/1934)
The State of Psychotherapy Today (1934)
Preface and Epilogue to "Essays on Contemporary
   Events" (1946)
Wotan (1936)
After the Catastrophe (1945)
The Fight with the Shadow (1946)
The Undiscovered Self (Present and Future) 1957)
Flying Saucers: A Modern Myth (1958)
A Psychological View of Conscience (1958)
Good and Evil in Analytical Psychology (1959)

Introduction to Wolff's "Studies in Jungian Psychology" (1959)
The Swiss Line in the European Spectrum (1928)
Reviews of Keyserling's "America Set Free" (1930) and "La Revolution Mondiale" (1934)
The Complications of American Psychology (1930)
The Dreamlike World of India (1939)
What India Can Teach Us (1939)
Appendix: Documents (1933-1938)

Vol. 11. PSYCHOLOGY AND RELIGION:
WEST AND EAST (1958, 1969)
WESTERN RELIGION
Psychology and Religion (The Terry Lectures)(1938/1940)
A Psychological Approach to the Dogma of the Trinity (1942/1948)
Transformation Symbolism in the Mass (1942/1954)
Forewords to White's "God and the Unconscious" and Werblowsky's "Lucifer and Prometheus" (1952)
Brother Klaus (1933)
Psychotherapists or the Clergy (1932)
Psychoanalysis and the Cure of Souls (1928)
Answer to Job (1952)
EASTERN RELIGION
Psychological Commentaries on "The Tibetan Book of the Great Liberation" (1939/1954) and "The Tibetan Book of the Dead" (1935/1953)
Yoga and the West (1936)
Foreward to Suzuki's "Introduction to Zen Buddhism" (1939)
The Psychology of Eastern Meditation (1943)
The Holy Men of India: Introduction to Zimmer's "Der Weg zum Selbst" (1944)
Foreward to the "I Ching" (1950)

Vol. 12 PSYCHOLOGY AND ALCHEMY (1944, 1953, 1968)
Prefatory note to the English Edition ([1951?] added 1967)
Introduction to the Religious and Psychological Problems of Alchemy

Individual Dream Symbolism in Relation to Alchemy (1936)
Religious Ideas in Alchemy (1937)
Epilogue

Vol. 13   ALCHEMICAL STUDIES (1968)
Commentary on "The Secret of the Golden Flower" (1929)
The Visions of Zosimos (1938/1954)
Paracelsus as a Spiritual Phenomenon (1942)
The Spirit Mercurius (1943/1948)
The Philosophical Tree (1945/1954)

Vol. 14.   MYSTERIUM CONIUNCTIONIS (1955-56, 1963, 1970)
AN INQUIRY INTO THE SEPARATION AND SYNTHESIS OF PSYCHIC OPPOSITES IN ALCHEMY
The Components of the Coniunctio
The Paradoxa
The Personification of the Opposites
Rex and Regina
Adam and Eve
The Conjunction

Vol. 15.   THE SPIRIT IN MAN, ART, AND LITERATURE (1966)
Paracelsus (1929)
Paracelsus the Physician (1941)
Sigmund Freud in His Historical Setting (1932)
In Memory of Sigmund Freud (1939)
Richard Wilhelm: In Memoriam (1930)
On the Relation of Analytical Psychology to Poetry (1922)
Psychology and Literature (1930/1950)
"Ulysses": A Monologue (1932)
Picasso (1932)

Vol. 16.   THE PRACTICE OF PSYCHOTHERAPY (1954, 1966)
GENERAL PROBLEMS OF PSYCHOTHERAPY
Principles of Practical Psychotherapy (1935)
What Is Psychotherapy? (1935)
Some Aspects of Modern Psychotherapy (1930)

The Aims of Psychotherapy (1931)
Problems of Modern Psychotherapy (1929)
Psychotherapy and a Philosophy of Life (1943)
Medicine and Psychotherapy(1945)
Psychotherapy Today (1945)
Fundamental Questions of Psychotherapy (1951)

SPECIFIC PROBLEMS OF PSYCHOTHERAPY
The Therapeutic Value of Abreaction (1921/1928)
The Practical Use of Dream-Analysis (1934)
The Psychology of the Transference (1946)
Appendix: The Realities of Practical Psychotherapy
([1937] added, 1966)

Vol. 17. THE DEVELOPMENT OF PERSONALITY (1954)
Psychic Conflicts in a Child (1910/1946)
Introduction to Wickes's "Analyses der Kinderseele"
(1927/1931)
Child Development and Education (1928)
Analytical Psychology and Education: Three Lectures
(1926/1946)
The Gifted Child (1943)
The Significance of the Unconscious in Individual
Education (1928)
The Development of Personality (1934)
Marriage as a Psychological Relationship (1925)

Vol. 18. THE SYMBOLIC LIFE (1976)
Miscellaneous Writings

Vol. 19. BIBLIOGRAPHY OF C. G. JUNG'S WRITINGS (1979)

Vol. 20. GENERAL INDEX TO THE COLLECTED WORKS
(1979)

Vol. A. ZOFINGIA LECTURES (supplement to the Collected
Works) edited by Wm. McGuire et al.

II.—OTHER WORKS BY C. G. JUNG

The Freud/Jung Letters; the Correspondence between Sigmund Freud and C. G. Jung. Edited by William McGuire. Princeton, N.J.: Princeton University Press, 1974.

C. G. Jung: Letters. Selected and edited by Gerhard Adler, in collaboration with Aniela Jaffe. Princeton, N.J.: Princeton University Press, 1973. Vol. 1 1906-1950; Vol. 2 1951-1961.

Carl G. Jung et al. *Man and His Symbols.* Garden City, N.Y.: Doubleday and Co., 1964.

C. G. Jung. *Memories, Dreams, Reflections.* Recorded and edited by Aniela Jaffe; translated from the German by Richard and Clara Winston. New York: Vintage Books, 1963.

C. G. Jung. *The Visions Seminars.* From the complete notes of Mary Foote. Postscript by Henry A. Murray. 2 vols. Spring Publications % Postfach 190, 8024 Zurich, Switzerland.

B. SECONDARY SOURCES AND WORKS CITED IN THE TEXT

Aristotle. *Basic Works.* Edited by Richard McKeon. New York: Random House, 1941.

Avens, Robert. *Imagination is Reality.* Irving, Texas: Spring Publications, 1980.

Ballard, Edward G. *Art and Analysis: An Essay Toward a Theory in Aesthetics.* The Hague: Martinus Nijhoff, 1957.

Ballard, Edward G. "On Ritual and Persuasion in Plato." *Southern Journal of Philosophy.* 11 (Summer 1964).

Banner, Robert. *Gothic Architecture.* New York: George Braziller, 1961.

BBC film. "The Story of C. G. Jung," told by Sir Laurens Van der Post. 1971.

Bertine, Eleanor. *Jung's Contribution to Our Time.* New York: published by Putnam for the C. G. Jung Foundation for Analytical Psychology, 1967.

Black, Max. *Models and Metaphors.* Ithaca: Cornell University Press, 1962.

Bloom, Benjamin S., Ed. *Taxonomy of Educational Objectives: The Classification of Educational Goals* Handbook I: Cognitive Domain by a Committee of College and University Examiners. New York: David McKay Co., 1956.

Bolen, Jean Shinoda. *Goddesses in Every Woman.* (New York: Harper and Row, 1984).

Brown, C.A. *Jung's Hermeneutic of Doctrine.* Chico, Calif.: Scholars Press, 1981).

Bryant, Christoper Rex. *Jung and the Christian Way.* New York: Seabury Press, 1984).

Buck, Percy C. *Oxford History of Music.* London: Oxford University Press, 1929.

Bukofzer, Manfred. *Studies in Medieval and Renaissance Music* New York: W.W. Norton and Co., 1950.

Cassirer, Ernest. *Language and Myth.* Trans. Susanne K. Langer. New York: Harper and Bros., 1946.

Castillejo, Irene Claremont de. *Knowing Woman: a Feminine Psychology.* New York: published by Putnam for the C. G. Jung Foundation for Analytical Psychology, 1973.

Clark, James. M. "C. G. Jung and Meister Eckhart." *Modern Language Review* 54 (1959). 239-44.

Clift, W.B. *Jung and Christianity: The Challenge of Reconciliation*. New York: Crossroads, 1982.

Conant, Kenneth John. *Carolingian and Romanesque Architecture, 800 to 1200*. Baltimore: Penquin Books, 1959.

Cooley, Rob. "Jung, Levi-Strauss and the Interpretation of Myth." *Criterion 8* (Autumn-Winter 1968-1979)12-16.

Conford, Francis. *From Religion to Philosophy*. New York: Longmans, Green and Co., 1912.

Coward, Harold. *Jung and Eastern Thought*. Albany, N.Y.: State University of New York, 1985.

Doran, Robert M. *Subject and Psyche: Ricoeur, Jung and the Search for Foundations*. Maryland: University Press of America, 1980.

Drury, Nevill. *Inner Visions: Explorations in Magical Consciousness*. London: Routledge & Kegal Paul, 1979.

Dufrenne, Mikel. *Language and Philosophy*. Bloomington: Indiana University Press, 1963.

Edinger, Edward. *The Creation of Consciousness: Jung's Myth for Modern Man*. Toronto: Inner City Books, 1984.

Edinger, Edward, "Christ as Paradigm of the Individuating Ego." *Spring* (1966)5-23.

Edinger, Edward F. *The Christian Archetypes: A Jungian Commentary on the Life of Christ*. Toronto: Inner City Books, 1987).

Edinger, Edward, F. Trinity and Quaternity. In *Der Archetyp. The Archetype. Proceedings of the 2d International Congress for Analytical Psychology*. Ed. Adolf Guggenbuhl-Craig. pp. 81-87. Basel and New York, 1964.

Ellenberger, Henri. *The Discovery of the Unconscious: The History and Evolution of Dynamic Psychiatry. London: Allen Lane, the*

Penguin Press, 1970.

Evans, Richard I. *Conversations with Carl Jung and Reactions from Ernest Jones.* Princeton: D. Van Nostrand Co., 1964.

Fordham, Michael. "The Evolution of Jung's Researches." *British Journal of Medical Psychology* 29 (1956) 3-8.

Fordham, Michael, *The Objective Psyche.* London: Routledge and Kegan Paul, 1958.

Fordham, Michael. *The Self in Jung's Writings.* Guild of Pastoral Psychology. Lecture no. 117. London, 1962a.

Fordham, Michael. "The Empirical Foundation and Theories of the Self in Jung's Work." *Journal of Analytical Psychology* 8, (1963) 1:1-23.

Franz, Marie Louise von. *C. G. Jung, His Myth in Our Time.* Boston: Little Brown, 1977.

Franz, Marie Louise von. *Number and Time: Reflections Leading Toward a Unification of Depth Psychology and Physics.* Evanston: Northwestern University Press, 1974.

Franz, Marie Louise von. *On Dreams and Death: A Jungian Interpretation.* Boston: Shambhala, 1986.

Franz, Marie Louise von. *Projection and Re-collection in Jungian Psychology; Reflections of the Soul.* LaSalle, Illinois: Open Court, 1980.

Friedman, Maurice. "Jung's Image of Psychological Man." *Psychoanalytic Review* 53 (1966-1967)4:595-608.

Hall, Everett W. *Philosophical Systems: A Categorial Analysis.* Chicago: University of Chicago Press, 1960.

Harding, Mary Esther. "Jung's Contribution to Religious Symbolism." *Spring* (1959) 1-16.

Harding, Mary Esther. *The "I" and the "Not I" A Study in the Development of Consciousness.* New York: Pantheon. 1965.

Harrow, Anita J. *A Taxonomy of the Psychomotor Domain: A Guide for Developing Behavioral Objectives.* New York: David McKay Co., 1972.

Heisig, James W. *Imago Dei: A Study of C. G. Jung's Psychology of Religion.* Lewisburg, Pa.: Bucknell University Press; London: Associated University Presses, 1979.

Hillman, James. *The Dream and the Underworld.* New York: Harper and Row, 1979.

Hillman, James, "The Feeling Function," *Lectures on Jung's Topology.* New York: Spring Publications, 1971.

Hillman, James. "Types, Images and the Vision of Completeness". New York: C. G. Jung Foundation, Audio Tape #012, 1977.

Hinkle, Beatice Moses. "Jung's Libido-Theory and the Bergsonian Philosophy." *New York Medical Journal* 99 (1919) 1080-86.

Hobson, Robert F. "Imagination and Amplification in Psychotherapy." *Journal of Analytical Psychology* 16, (1971). 1:79-105.

Hugh, Dom Anselm. "Early Medieval Music up to 1300" *New Oxford History of Music.* Vol. 11 London: Oxford University Press, 1954.

Jacobi, Jolande. *Complex, Archetype, Symbol in the Psychology C. G. Jung.* New York: Pantheon Books. 1959.

Jacobi, Jolande. *The Way of Individuation.* London: Hodder and Stoughton, 1967.

Jaffé, Aniela. *Apparitions and Precognition: a Study from the Point of View of C. G. Jung's Analytical Psychology.* New Hyde Park, N.Y.: University Books, 1963.

Jaffé, Aniela. "The Creative Phases in Jung's Life." *Spring* (1972). 162-90.

Jaffé, Aniela. *From the Life and Work of C. G. Jung.* London: Hodder and Stoughton, 1971.

Jaffé, Aniela. *The Myth of Meaning in the Work of C. G. Jung.* London: Hodder and Stoughton, 1970.

Jahoda, Gustav. "Jung's Meaningful Coincidences." *The Philosophical Journal* 4 (1967) 35-42.

Jantz, Harold. "Goethe, Faust, Alchemy and Jung." *German Quarterly* 35 (1962) 129-41.

Kant, Immanuel. *Critique of Pure Reason.* Trans. Norman Kemp Smith. New York: St. Martin's Press, Inc., 1961.

Kawai, H. *Professor Carl G. Jung and Japanese Psychology.* Kyoto: Psychologia, 1961.

Kelsey, Morton. "Jung as Philosopher and Theologian." In Hilda Kirsch, ed., *The Well-Tended Tree: Essays into the Spirit of our Times.* New York: G. P. Putnam's Sons, 1971, 184-96.

Krathwohl, David R.; Benjamin S. Bloom and Bertram B. Masia. *Taxonomy of Educational Goals* Handbook II: Affective Domain. New York; David McKay Co., 1964.

Lambert, Kenneth. "Jung's Later Work: Historical Studies." *British Journal of Medical Psychology.* 35 (1962) 3:191-97

Langer, Susanne K. *Feeling and Form.* New York, 1953

Langer, Susanne K. *Mind: An Essay on Human Feeling.* Baltimore: John Hopkins Press, 1967, Vol. 1.

Langer, Susanne K. *Problems of Art: Ten Philosophical Lectures.* New York: Charles Scribner's Sons, 1957.

220

Lewis Aubrey. "Jung's Early Work." *Journal of Analytical Psychology* 2 (1957) 2: 119-35.

Lewis, C.I. "The Given Element in Empirical Knowledge." *Philosophical Review* LXI (April 1952).

Lewis, C.I. *Mind and World Order: Outline for a Theory of Knowledge.* New York: Charles Scribner's Sons, 1929.

McGuire, William. *Bollingen: an Adventure in Collecting the Past.* Princeton N.J.: Princeton University Press, 1982.

McGuire, William, and R.F.C. Hull, eds. *C. G. Jung Speaking; Interviews and Encounters.* Princeton, N.J.: Princeton University Press. 1977.

McLeish, John. "Carl Jung, Psychology and Catholicism." *Wiseman Review* 489 (Fall 1961); 264-76; 490 (Winter 1961-62): 313-18.

McLuhan, Marshall, *Understanding Media; The Extensions of Man.* New York: McGraw-Hill Book Co., 1964.

Mairet, Philip. "Presuppositions of Psychological Analysis." In *Christian Essays in Psychiatry.* London: SCM Press. 1056, 40-72.

Malone, Michael. *Psycho-types.* New York: Dutton, 1977.

Mann, Harriet; Miriam Siegler, and Humphrey Asmond, "The Many Worlds of Time." *Journal of Analytical Psychology* (January 1968).

Meier, Carl Alfred. "Projection, Transference and the Subject-Object Relation in Psychology." *Journal of Analytical Psychology* 4 (1959a) 1:21-34.

Moore, Charles Herbert. *Development and Character of Gothic Architecture.* London: Macmillan and Co., 1890.

Moreno, Antonio. *Jung, Gods and Modern Man.* Notre Dame, Indiana: University of Notre Dame Press, 1970.

Moses, Paul J. "The Psychology of the Castrato Voice," *International Journal of Phoniatry,* XII, 3, 204-216.

Neumann, Erich. *Art and the Creative Unconscious.* New York: Pantheon Books, 1959.

Neumann, Erich. *Creative Man.* Princeton, N.J.: Princeton University Press, 1979.

Neumann, Erich, *The Origins and History of Consciousness.* Princeton, N.J.: Princeton University Press, 1970.

Onians, R.B. *Origins of European Thought about the Body, the Mind, the Soul, the World, Time and Fate.* Cambridge, England, 1954

The Oxford Annotated Bible. New York: Oxford University Press, 1962.

Philip, Howard L. *Jung and the Problem of Evil.* London: Salisbury Square, 1958.

Plato, The Collected Dialogues Including the Letters, edited by Edith Hamilton and Huntington Cairnes; Bollingen Series LXXI. New York: Pantheon Books, 1966.

Plotinus, *Complete Works,* ed. by Kenneth Sylvan Guthrie. Comparative Literature Press, 1918, 4 vols.

Price, H.H. "Review of Jung and Pauli," *Naturerklärung und Psyche. Journal of the Society for Psychical Research* 37 (1953). 26-35.

Progroff, Ira. *The Death and Rebirth of Psychology; an Integrative Evaluation of Freud, Adler, Jung, and Rank and the Impact of Their Culminating Insights on Modern Man.* New York: Julian Press, 1956.

Progroff, Ira. *Depth Psychology and Modern Man.* New York: Julian Press, 1954.

Progroff, Ira. *Jung, Synchronicity, and Human Destiny: Non Causal Dimensions of Human Experience.* New York: Julian Press, 1973.

Progroff, Ira. *Jung's Psychology and Its Social Meaning.* New York: Grove Press, 1953.

Progroff, Ira. *The Symbolic and the Real; a New Psychological Approach to the Fuller Experience of Personal Existence.* New York: McGraw-Hall, 1973.

Reichenbach, Hans. "Are Phenomenal Reports Absolutely Certain?" *Philosophical Review.* LXI (April 1952).

Reichenbach, Hans. *Experience and Prediction.* Chicago: University of Chicago Press, 1952.

Rhine, J.B. *Extra-Sensory Perception.* Boston, 1934.

Rist, John M,. "Plotinus on Matter and Evil. "*Phonesis* 6 (1961) 154-66.

Samuels, Andrew. *Jung and the Post-Jungians.* London; Boston: Routledge and Kegan Paul, 1985.

Sanford, John A. "Analytical Psychology: Science or Religion? An Exploration of the Epistemology of Analytical Psychology." In Hilda Kirsch, ed. *The Well-Tended Tree: Essays into the Spirit of Our Times.* New York: G.P. Putman's Sons, 1971, 90-105.

Simpson, Elizabeth Jane. *The Classification of Educational Objectives: Psychomotor Domain.* University of Illinois Research Project No. OE-5-85-104, 1966.

Staude, John-Raphael. *The Adult Development of C. G. Jung.* Boston: Routledge and Kegan Paul, 1981.

Urban, Wilbur Marshall. *Beyond Realism and Idealism*. London: Allen and Unwin, 1949.

Van der Post, Laurens. *Jung and the Story of Our Time*. New York: Pantheon Books, 1975.

Whitehead, Alfred N. *Science and the Modern World*. New York: The Free Press, 1967.

Wooldridge, H.E. *The Oxford History of Music*. London: Oxford University Press, 1929, Vol. 1: *The Polyphonic Period*.

ABOUT THE ILLUSTRATORS

Betty Burke is Art Historian for the Nortolk City public schools.

Lorraine Fink is a painter and teacher in the Tidewater Area.

Henry Reed is a psychologist and dream researcher in Virginia Beach.

Fay Zetlin is Artist-in-Residence at Old Dominion University.

A

Acausal connection of events, 34
Affect
  definition of, 50
  orchestration of, 50
Anima archetype
  projected in Gothic cathedrals, 101
  projected in Roman Christian church,
    99
  projected in Romanesque churches,
    101
Anima tension, 98, 99
Animus archetype
  projected in Gothic cathedrals, 101
  projected in Roman Christian church,
    99
Animus pole 97-98
"Answer to Job" (Jung), 85, 87, 140
Antimonies, psyche's need for, 191
A priori, 13-27
  Jung's view of, 34-35
  views of contemporary philosophers,
    13
Archetypes, 9, 17, 56
  anima/animus archetypes, 97-101
  a priori of psyche and, 34-35
  autonomy of, 36
  Christian myth of love and union,
    75-76
  content of, 97
  function of, 46
  human symbols used to study, 97
  instinct and, 46
  numinosities of, 65-66
  ordered sequences of, 39
  of soul, 180
  spirit as archetype of creative
    process, 46
  spontaneous images and, 55
  sun and moon as archetypal energies
    in Seven Days of Creation, 169
  unus mundus and, 87
Archetypes and the Collective
  Unconscious (Jung), 15-16
Aristotle, 117, 157
Artist
  creativity and, 47-48, 57
  as instrument of transcendent power,
    54
Art media
  evolution of, 94
  structures in, 91-104
  tensions, 92
  transformation of, 92-93
Art symbols, 91
Avens, Robert, 69

B

Baroque period
  emergence of castrato voice, 103
  musical revolution of, 103-4
Bergson, Henri, 5, 9
Black, Max, 13
Bloom, Benjamin S., 107, 115
Break boundary, art media and, 94
Breuer, Joseph, 6
Burckhardt, Jakob, 4

C

Carus, C. G., 6
Cassirer, Ernst, 10, 23, 26-27
Castrato voice
  emergence of, 103
  godlike character of, 104
  Orfeo and, 104
Children, psychological types and, 117
Cognitive skills, feeling type child
  and, 117
Collective unconscious, 9, 46, 56
  limits of, 96
  soul as mediator between conscious
    ego life and, 49
  unus mundus and, 87
Conscience
  as divine intervention, 72
  inner voice and, 70-71
  justification of, 71
  as undoubted dynamism, 73
Consciousness, 56
  darkness and, 82
  interference in psyche, 51-52
  Jung's definition of, 46
  limitation in space and time, 141
  of the unconscious, 169-70
  Western versus Eastern
    consciousness, 73-74
Cornford, Francis, 23, 26-27

Correspondence of formal elements, in media, 104
Creation, as transformation, 162
Creation myths
  psyche and, 145
  as symbolic records of consciousness, 145
Creativity, 45-57
  artist and, 47-48, 57
  compelling nature of, 47
  cooperation with creative process, 48
  darkness and, 82
  electing to be uncreative, 151-52
  essence of, 62
  First Day of Creation and, 150-51
  function in art, 49-50
  as "Ground of the Psyche", 49
  as instinct, 45-46
  Jung's concept of, 46-48
  selectivity of, 151
  spirit and, 45-47
  time needed by, 152
Critique of Judgment (Kant), 15
Critique of Practical Reason (Kant), 15
Critique of Pure Reason (Kant), 3, 14, 25
Crookes, William, 4

D
Darkness
  consciousness and, 82
  creative process and, 82
  Jungian perspective of, 82
Death
  life after, 141, 142
  positive meaning of, 130
  rebirth symbols, 142
  rest of Seventh Day as, 184
  significance to educational process, 130
Differentiated consciousness, 198
Divine intervention, 140
  conscience as, 72
Divine Mind, Plotinus' view of, 80
Divine Soul
  actuation of, 81
  as psyche, 80

"The Dream and the Underworld" (Hillman), 69
Dreams of a Spirit Seer (Kant), 4
Dufrenne, Mikel, 13
Duprel, Karl, 4

E
Eckhart, Meister, as philosophical mentor, 2
Educational process
  affective domain, 107
    classification of objectives of, 107-8
  death's significance to, 130
  development of feeling function, 116-17
  development of intuitive function, 119-20
  development of sensation function, 118-19
  development of thinking function, 116
  ego formation, 120
  in mature years, 123-31
    college/university enrollments, 126
    goal setting, 129-30
    lack of awareness of education needs, 127
    needs for further education, 125
    and significance of later life, 128
    recognition of type by educators, 120-21
  thinking and, 115
Ego formation, educational process, 120
Einstein, Albert, 32-33
Emotion, conscience and, 70
Empedocles, 2
Ennead (Plotinus), 80, 81
Eros-thanatos tension, 23
Eternity, psyche and, 141-42
Evil, 194
  evil soul, 81
  as a form, 80
  Gnostic view of, 83
  as manifestation of dark side of God, 84-85

mystery of, 81-82
Plotinus' view of, 79-81
Extra-sensory perception, Jung's
    interest in, 141
Extraverted sensation child, 116

F
Fate, *See* Gods.
Faust (Goethe), 2
    compared to *Thus Spake Zarathustra*,
    4
Feeling type, 110-11
    auxiliary functions of, 115
    development of, 116-17
    extraverted feeling, 110
    influence on others, 111
    introverted feeling, 110
    motivations, 110
    poetry and, 111
    taught forms of feeling, 116-17
    time and, 110-11
"Final view", 36
Flournoy, Theodore, 5
Freud, Sigmund, 23
    importance to Jung, 5, 6
Fringe of consciousness, 64

G
Gifted feeling-type child, 116
Gnostics
    dualism of Gnostic systems, 84
    view of evil, 83
God
    as amoral masculine being, 85
    involvement in dynamics of his
        creation, 85-86
    Job as witness to dark side of, 85
God-image, as human projection, 87, 88
Gods
    aspiring to realm of, 65
    cooperation with, 67
Goethe, Johann Wolfgang von, 2, 4, 82
Golden mean, concept of, 117-18
Gothic cathedrals
    interior design, 101
    music, 103
        sygzy, 103
    projection of anima, 101
    projection of animus, 101

projection of tension, 101

H
Hall, Everett W., 13
Hegel, Georg Wilhelm Friedrich, as
    philosophical mentor, 2, 5
Heraclitus, 2
Hermaphrodite, in Jungian psychology,
    103
Hermeneutic method, 56, 193
    lifelines constructed by, 53-54
    of understanding spontaneous images,
        52-53
Hillman, James, 69
Human symbols, used to study
    archetypes, 97
Hyperkinetic children, 116, 119

I
Ideational mandalas, 22
Images
    negative images, 83
    as projections of higher self, 83
    spontaneous images, 52-55
        archetypes and, 55
        connection between events and, 55
        inexplicability of, 54
        understanding of, 52-53
    symbols found in, 63
Imaginal versus concrete, 69
Imagination, myths of creation and, 61-
    62
"Imagination Is Reality" (Avens), 69
Individuation, 145
    essential elements of, 73-74
        integration, 73-74
        objective relationship, 74
    and need for education, 126-27
    Universal Soul and, 80
Inferior functions, development of,
    119-20, 125
Inherited ideas, 15
Inner voice
    conscience and, 70-71
    obedience to, 72
    as voice of God, 72
Instinct, 56
    archetypes and, 46
    creativity as, 45-46

Jung's view of, 45-46
Interior design
  Roman Christian church, 99
  Romanesque church, 100-101
"The Interpretation of Nature and the
  Psyche" (Jung/Pauli), 10
Introverted intuitive child, 116
Intuitive type, 113-14
  education of 119-20
  neglect of, 120
  See Irrational functions
Irrational functions, 123-24
  intuitive type, 113
    auxiliary functions of, 115
    indifference to objects, 113-14
    morality and, 113
    sensation of intuitive type, 113
    stable conditions and, 113
    time and, 114
    transmission of images by, 113
  sensation type, 111-13
    disadvantage of type, 113
    extraverted sensation-type, 111
    introverted sensation-type, 111-
      12
    others' feelings and, 112
    practicality of, 112
    sense perception, 112

J
James, William, 5, 64
  fringe of consciousness, 64
Janet, Pierre, 5, 6
Job, 180
  as witness to dark side of God, 85
Jung, C. G.
  alchemy and, 7-8
  analysis of uniting symbols, 15
  anima/animus, 97-101
  antimonies of, 24-25, 26
  apprenticeship at Burghulzli Mental
    Hospital, 5, 135
  a priori and, 13-27
  archetypes, 9, 15-17, 36, 39, 56,
    75-76, 97-101, 169, 180
  attraction to science, 3-4
  Collected Works, xiii
  on collective a priori beneath

personal psyche, 137
  conception of method of
    psychotherapy, 190, 191-92
  confrontation with the unconscious,
    7-8
  on conscience, 71-74
  on consciousness, 10, 46, 56, 141,
    169-70
  on creativity, 45-57
  on darkness, 82
  dreams of, 135-37, 141
  early childhood, 2, 133-34
  on educational process, 107-121
    in mature years, 123-31
  Einstein and, 32-33
  as empiricist, 189
  epistemology, 189
  on evil, 80-85
  Gnosticism and neo-Platonism, 8, 10
  Goethe as philosophical mentor, 2
  human personality, conceptual model
    of, 123
  individuation,, xi-xii, 73-74,
    126-27, 145
  on instinct, 45-46, 56
  on kinship libido, 74-75
  mandalas, 6, 20-22
  on meaning, 40-41, 196, 202-3
  on metaphysics, 31-32
  metaphysics of, 86-88, 87
  on morality, 69-70
  mysticism of, 79, 86, 133-43, 199
    religious manifestation, 139
  on natural numbers, 37-40
  on number two personality, 137-38
  origins of language symbolism, 26
  performed patterns of apperception,
    15-16
  philosophical development, 2-5
  philosophical mentors, 1-11
  philosophy, xiii
  philosophy of creativity, 45-57
  philosophy versus mysticism, 199-200
  professorship at University of
    Zurich, 5-6
  on psyche, 18-19, 35, 66-67, 145
  psychological functions, 108
    space-time orientation, 108

on psychotherapy, 190-93
reality of evil to, 82-85
reality of God to, 82-83, 85-86
school years, 3-4
search for answers to Christian
    theological questions, 82
search for knowledge, xi
self-criticism, 203
on soul, 48-49
    as mediator between collective
        unconscious and conscious
        ego life, 49
on source of knowledge, 11
space and time, 35-36
spiritualism, attraction to, 4
on spiritualistic phenomena, 134-35
on spirituality, 67-69
structures in art media, 91-104
student years, 134
synchronicity, 31-42
theory of humanity, 194
understanding of feminine psyche,
    199
on uniting symbols, 19-20, 27
unus mundus, 87, 88
view of education, 195
    special needs for education in
        mature years, 195
view of love, 200-201
world view, as reflection of
    Einstein's notion of
    relativity, 10
Jungian psychology, Apollinian
    emphasis in, 65
Justification of conscience, 71

K
Kant, Immanuel, 4, 13, 14, 87
    antinomies of pure reason, 24-25, 26
        resolution of, 25
    delineation of *a priori,* 14-15
    on metaphysics, 31
    as philosophical mentor, 3
Karma, Jung's view of, 143
Kerner, Justinus, 4
Kinship libido, 74-75
    as foundation of morality, 75
    satisfaction of, 75

"Krug's General Dictionary of the
    Philosophical Sciences", 2, 6
L
Langer, Susanne, 91-104, 158
Lao-Tzu, 8
Lewis, C. I., 13
Liebniz, 6
Life after death, *See* Death, life
    after.
Lifelines, 53, 56
Logic of the imagination, 118

M
Machaut, Guillaume de, 103
McLuhan, Marshall, 91-104
Mandalas
    drawing of, 6
    as symbol of wholeness, 20-22
    as uniting symbols, 22
"Marriage as a Psychological
    Relationship" (Jung), 75
Matter
    as Evil, 80, 81
    inclination of soul toward, 81
Mature years
    educational process, 123-31
        college/university enrollments,
            126
        goal setting, 129-30
        lack of awareness of education
            needs, 127
        needs for further education, 125
        and significance of later life,
            128
Meaning
    a priori condition for finding, 40-
        41
    discovery of, 41
    myth of, 196, 202-3
"Meaningful coincidence", 33, 42
Media, interaction among, 94
"Memories, Dreams, Reflections" (Jung),
    67-69, 82
Metaphorical symbols, 91-92
Metaphysics
    relevancy of synchronicity to, 41
    similarities between Plotinus and
        Jung, 86-88

Whitehead on, 31-32
Mind: An Essay of Human Feeling (Langer), 91
Monad
  self as, 6-7
  use of term, 6
Moral function, spontaneous images and, 53
Morality, 69
  conscience and, 70-72
  in creative life, 70-71
  inner voice and, 72
  Jung's definition of, 69-70
  kinship libido as foundation of, 75
  origin of moral laws, 70
  See also Conscience.
Music
  Baroque period, 103-4
  castrato voice, emergence of, 103
  Gothic cathedrals, 103
  sygyzy, 103
  Roman Christian church, 100
  Romanesque churches, 101
Mysticism, 133-43
  current definition of, 133
  Jung's religious manifestation of, 139
  leading to theory of synchronicity, 140-41
Myths, 196, 197

N
Natural numbers
  Chinese conception of, 40
  number eleven, 39
  number four, 39
  number three, 38-39
  number two, 38
  primal one, 38
  synchronicity and, 37-40
Negative images, as "shadow", 83-84
Nicomachean Ethics (Aristotle), 117-18
Nietzsche, Friedrich Wilhelm, 4-5
  intuition of, 5
Nous, Plotinus' view of, 80
Number two personality
  Jung's awareness of, 137-38
    home as expression of, 139

Numinosity, of archetypes, 65-66

O
Objective relationships, psychological counterpart, 74
One, Plotinus' view of, 79-81
Onians, R. B., 23
Ordered sequences, of archetypes, 39
Orfeo, castrato voice and, 104

P
Participation mystique, 23, 63-64
  primitive thinking and, 64
Passavant, J. K., 4
Pauli, Wolfgang, 10
Perception, 34
  conditioned by *a priori* structure of psyche, 16-17
  perceptual motor programs, basis of, 107-8
  sense perception of introverted sensation-type, 112
  thinking function, 108
Personality number two
  Jung's awareness of, 137-38
  home as expression of, 139
Plato, 2, 10, 22, 143
Plotinus, 148
  on evil, 79-88
  metaphysics of 81, 86-87
  mysticism of, 79
  unity of the One, 79
Poetics (Aristotle), 157
Polarity, 52
Power, 201
Primitive mode of perception, 64-65
Primordial images
  affect and, 50
  in soul, 49-50
  ground of, 50
Privatio boni, 83, 85, 88
Problem children, psychological types and, 117
Psi-phenomena, 34, 35
  archetypes and, 35
Psyche, 17-18
  a priori of, 34-35
  bridge between nature and, 36-37
  creation myths and, 145

development of, 18-19
Divine Soul as, 80
eternity and, 141-42
gaining knowledge of, 66-67
Jung's conception of, 35
need for antimonies, 191
qualitative dimension of, 35
Psychic processes, tendency toward
rhythmical expression, 40
Psychoid level, soul at, 54
Psychological types, 108
fourth function, development of,
120-21, 124, 170-71
innate tendency toward type, 114
inner and outer aspects of, 108-9
predominant function, 124
pure types, 114
relation to educational endeavors,
124
See also Irrational functions;
Rational functions.
"A Psychological View of Conscience"
(Jung), 70
"Psychology of the Child Archetype"
(Jung), 18-19
"The Psychology of the Transference"
(Jung), 73-74, 75
Psychotherapy
creative process of, 192-93
as dialectical process, 190-91
greatest healing power in, 191-92
Pythagoras, 2
R
Rational functions, 123
feeling type, 110-11
extraverted feeling, 110
influence on others, 111
introverted feeling, 110
motivations, 110
poetry and, 111
time and, 110-11
thinking type, 109-10
extraverted thinking, 109
flow of process and, 109
introverted thinking, 109
ordering of reality and, 110
spontaneity, 110
temporal orientation, 110

Rational mode, integrated life and, 64-65
Rebirth symbols, in those approaching
death, 142
Reichenbach, Hans, 13
Reincarnation, Jung's view of, 143
Relativity principle, world view of, 32
Religion
belief in God, 139-40
death and, 142-43
as manifestation of Jung's
mysticism, 139
mystery at core of, 140
Rhine, J. B., 141
"The Role of the Unconscious" (Jung),
15
Roman Christian church
colors, 99
interior design, 99
movement within, 99
music, 100
sygyzy, 100
as projection of anima archetype, 99
as projection of animus archetype,
99
Romanesque church
interior design, 100-101
music, 101
projection of anima, 100
unity symbols, 101
S
Schopenhauer, Arthur, as philosophical
mentor, 2-3, 5
Second soul, 81
The Secret of the Golden Flower,
6
Self
as archetype of orientation and
meaning, 8
as inner experience, 1
primal one and, 38
Self knowledge, 180
Sensation type, 111-13
auxiliary functions of, 115
disadvantage of type, 113
extraverted sensation-type, 111
introverted sensation-type, 111-12
others' feelings and, 112

practicality of, 112
sense perception, 112
Seven Days of Creation, 145-86
  Fifth Day, 173-75
    birds, 173-74
    fish, 173-74
    gaining access to one's creative
      powers, 174-75
    great sea monsters, 173
  First Day, 147-52
    affirmation of will, 149
    duality, 148
    God as *Imago Dei,* 147-48
    implication of initial stage of
      creative process, 150
    inspiration, 148-49
    moral integrity, 150
    potentiality, 148
    transcendence, 150
    unfathomable deep, 149
  Fourth Day, 167-68
    as advanced creativity, 169
    light, 167-68
    stars as projection of
      collective unconscious,
      168-69, 170-71
    as ongoing development of
      consciousness, 147
    as path of individuation, 185-86
  Second Day, 155-59
    firmament as perspective, 155,
      157
    higher waters, 156-58
    ideal order of reality, 158
    lower waters, 156
    refining of movement and
      direction in creativity, 158
    waters as potentialities of
      spirit and nature, 158-59
  Seventh Day, 183-84
    blessedness of, 183-84
    as completion of cycle of birth
      and death, 185
    rest as death, 184
  Sixth Day, 177-80
    creation of animal and human
      life, 178
    governing nature, 179-80

humans in God's image, 178-79
human's possessions, 179
individual's power in universe,
  180
nurturing, 179-80
Third Day, 161-64
  accomplishment, 163-64
  dry land appearing out of lower
    waters, 161-62
  vegetation, 162-63
Sexuality, cosmic nature of, 179
Shadow, 194
  feelings at shadow pole, 98
  negative images as, 83-84
Shadow-transcendence tension, in early
  Christian art, 99
Slow learners, psychological types and,
  117
Smith, Norman Kemp, 14
Sophia, as unconscious wisdom, 85, 86
Soul, 56, 57
  archetypes of, 180
  at psychoid level, 54
  evil, 81
  inclination toward matter, 81
  irrational part of, 80
  Jung's view of, 48-49
    as mediator between collective
      unconscious and conscious
      ego life, 49
    as mediator between conscious ego
      life and collective
      unconscious, 49
  as "physical aspect of matter", 55
  primordial images in, 49-50
  second soul, 81
  Universal Soul, 80
  unus mundus and, 87
Space and time
  elimination of by electric
    technology, 94-95
  transcendence of, 141
Spirit, 56
  as archetype of creative process,
    46
  cooperation with individual, 45
  creativity and, 45-47
Spiritualistic phenomena, influence on

Jung, 134-35
Spirituality, oriental spirituality
    compared to Jung's view, 67-69
Spontaneous images
    archetypes and, 55
    connection between events and, 55
    inexplicability of, 54
    understanding of, 52-53
The Story of C. G. Jung (Van der Post),
    133
Suzuki, D. T., 69
Swedenborg, Emanuel, 4
Sygyzy, 97
    hermaphrodite as symbol of, 103
    in music of early Roman Christian
        church, 100
    in music of Gothic cathedrals, 103
    in music of Romanesque church, 101
Symbols
    overly symbolic life, warning about,
        65
    psychic manifestations of, 63
    roots of, 91-104
Synchronicity, 31-42, 87, 198
    acausal connection of events, 34
    characteristics of, 32-37
    Jung's use of term, 33-34
    mysticism leading to theory of, 140-
        41
    pervasiveness in universe, 37
    relevancy to metaphysics, 41
    synchronistic phenomena, 55, 57

T
Tao
    compared to Christianity, 9
    concept of, 8-9
Taxonomy of Educational Objectives
    (Bloom), 107
Tensions
    released through uniting symbols,
        22-23
    structures in art media, 92
Thinking type, 109-10
    auxiliary functions of, 115
    extraverted thinking, 109
    flow of process and, 109
    introverted thinking, 109

    ordering of reality and, 110
    spontaneity, 110
    temporal orientation, 110
Thinking type child, 116
Thoughts Out of Season (Nietszche), 4
Three-dimensional world
    space and time in, 35-36
    understanding of psyche and, 37
Thus Spake Zarathustra (Nietszche), 4-5
Transcendent function, 51

U
Unconscious
    consciousness of, 169-70
    uniting of spirit and instinct in,
        46
Union of opposites, Jung's
    interpretation of, 7
Uniting symbols, 19-20, 27
    appearance of, 19-20
    Jung's definition of, 20
    psyche development and, 18-20
    tensions released through, 22-23
Universal Soul
    individuation and, 80
    Plotinus' view of, 80
Unus mundus
    archetypes and, 87
    psyche and physis in, 87

V
Van der Post, Sir Laurens, 133
Von Eschenmayer, K.A. von, 4
von Franz, Dr. Marie-Louise, 38-41
von Gorres, J., 4
von Hartmann, Eduard, 4, 6

W
Whitehead, Alfred N., 31
Wilhelm, Richard, 6
Wisdom, gaining of, 67
Wittengenstein, 193

Z
Zoellner, Friedrich, 4

Joachim Jung

SUBJEKTIVE ÄSTHETIK

New Studies in Aesthetics. Vol. 1

ISBN 0-8204-0519-1   462 pages   hardback US $ 58.00*

*Recommended price – alterations reserved

Das vorliegende Werk enthält ein neues ästhetisches System, das auf der spe-
zifischen Empfindung des Einzelnen beruht. Während die Subjektivität in der
klassischen Ästhetik immer künstlich nivelliert und in eine objektive Gesetz-
mäßigkeit verwandelt wurde, orientiert sich Jung an der tatsächlichen Persön-
lichkeit, die von individuellen Anlagen und kulturellen Einflüssen geprägt
wird. Der Autor vermeidet eine Überbewertung der Kontemplation, indem
er die Rolle der künstlerischen Gestaltung hervorhebt: das Anschauen und
das Schaffen, der Betrachter und das Genie werden als gleichberechtigte
Komplementärphänomene anerkannt. Dabei beschränkt sich diese Abhand-
lung nicht nur auf die Erörterung ästhetischer Probleme, sondern eröffnet
auch den Blick auf eine Weltanschauung, die immer wieder die Singularität
und Eigenart des Individuums herausstellt und damit zur Erhellung wesentli-
cher Probleme der menschlichen Existenz beiträgt.

« The book is an admirably thorough and well-thought out study of the subjective from the aesthetic point of view. Such a topic is really central to the field
of aesthetics, yet contemporary scholars and theorists either shy away from it
or else take it for granted. Jung opens up the topic to fullscale philosophical
analysis. He offers us an impressive return to the foundations of aesthetics.»
(Robert Ginsberg, The Pennsylvania State University)

PETER LANG PUBLISHING, INC.
62 West 45th Street
USA – New York, NY 10036

Ernest Joós

POETIC TRUTH AND TRANSVALUATION IN NIETZSCHE'S ZARATHUSTRA

American University Studies: Series V (Philosophy). Vol. 31

ISBN 0-8204-0432-4   200 pages   hardback US $ 28.00*

*Recommended price – alterations reserved

Heidegger wanted to take Nietzsche seriously as a thinker. But as a thinker or philosopher Nietzsche can be accused of inconsistency. Even his main objective – *the transvaluation of all values* – may make no sense. This author wants to view Nietzsche as a poet. He opposes the universality of abstract truth to the *poetic truth* which is the incarnation of the absolute in the concrete and valid only as *meaning* in a particular context. A large part of the book is devoted to the application of this theory, hence the book is both a hermeneutic study and a practical guide for the interpretation of Nietzsche's controversial topics such as the Death of God, marriage, life and death, or – women and the Superman *(Übermensch)*. Part Three deals with Hermeneutics and Metaphysics, then with Heidegger, Nietzsche and Metaphysics.

PETER LANG PUBLISHING, INC.
62 West 45th Street
USA – New York, NY 10036

Robin Robertson

C. G. JUNG AND THE ARCHETYPES OF THE COLLECTIVE UNCONSCIOUS

American University Studies: Series (Psychology). Vol. 7

ISBN 0-8204-0395-4   272 pages   hardback US $ 30.50*

*Recommended price – alterations reserved

The author presents a stimulating panorama of Jung's psychology, and shows how accurately it corresponds to the strange world described by twentieth-century scientists in fields other than psychology. He traces the development of the concept of the archetypes of the collective unconscious from the dawn of the scientific method in the Renaissance to twentieth-century mathematician Kurt Gödel's proof of the limits of science. Robertson's presentation of Jung's psychology is the most complete to date, treating it as a connected whole, from the early experimental studies to the final work using alchemy as a model of psychological dynamics.

Contents: A panorama of Jung's psychology, tracing a history of ideas from the Renaissance to 20th century mathematics – For both the intelligent general reader and the specialist on Jung.

 PETER LANG PUBLISHING, INC.
62 West 45th Street
USA – New York, NY 10036